D0043697

ARE WE COMPATIBLE?

C.E. Rollins

OLIVER NELSON

THOMAS NELSON PUBLISHERS
Nashville • Atlanta • London • Vancouver

Copyright © 1995 by Jan L. Dargatz

All rights reserved. Written permission must be secured from the publisher to use or reproduce any part of this book, except for brief quotations in critical reviews or articles.

Published in Nashville, Tennessee, by Thomas Nelson, Inc., Publishers, and distributed in Canada by Word Communications, Ltd., Richmond, British Columbia.

The Bible version used in this publication is THE NEW KING JAMES VERSION. Copyright © 1979, 1980, 1982, Thomas Nelson, Inc., Publishers.

Library of Congress Cataloging-in-Publication Data

Rollins, Catherine E., 1950–
    Are we compatible? / C.E. Rollins.
      p. cm.
    ISBN 0-7852-8000-6 (pbk.)
    1. Mate selection. 2. Marriage. 3. Marriage compatibility tests. I. Title.
HQ801.R65   1995
646.7'7—dc20   94-23156
                                              CIP

Printed in the United States of America.

1 2 3 4 5 6 — 00 99 98 97 96 95

To
Rena, Jeff, and Christi
with high hopes that each of you
will find a compatible mate

CONTENTS

PREFACE

For nearly fifteen years, I worked as a teacher and administrator at a small private university, during which time I had the opportunity to converse and counsel with hundreds—if not thousands—of students who were in various stages of romantic relationships: "just friends," newly dating, seriously dating, engaged, newly married, and recently divorced.

I noticed two major common threads in those relationships that seemed the healthiest and that resulted in the strongest marriages through the years: (1) a strong commitment to marriage itself, as opposed to a strong attraction to the other person in the relationship, and (2) a strong foundation of similarities in background, temperament, goals and dreams, values, and the ways in which individuals managed and ordered their physical and material lives. This latter set of similarities I regard as compatibility.

"How might two people determine in advance of their marriage vows if they are compatible?" That question led to the development of the "Compatibility Model" and compatibility tests presented in this book.

Primarily, I was looking for a way that would visualize for both parties, who tended to be looking at life and their relationship with rose-colored glasses, those areas in which they were very similar and those in which they were quite dissimilar—not to persuade them to dissolve their relationship but to see in advance of marriage where the difficult spots were likely to be in their relationship and then to develop means of addressing and resolving those difficulties. As one young man put it after a seminar on compatibility, "We now know where the alligators are in the swamp, and we've got training in dealing with them."

A good marriage is a highly precious thing—perhaps the greatest relationship a person can experience this side of heaven. Good marriages are to be treasured and sought.

"Just being married" isn't enough. A mediocre or bad marriage can lead to tremendous frustration, bitterness, and a host of other unhealthy emotions for both people involved. We need strong marriages—ones that will endure and provide joy, fulfillment, and good role models for the coming generations. This book is intended to help people who are considering marriage to take a realistic look at who they are and how they relate in hopes that they will, in turn, have the skills to create strong marriages. The key to a good marriage relationship lies in being compatible, not just being in love.

The stories told here have been altered slightly in detail, and the names changed, to protect the privacy of the individuals and couples—but the principles and situations are real. Compatibility is real. It is possible. It is achievable.

May you find compatibility not only on these pages but in your life!

—C. E. Rollins

Chapter 1

WHAT DOES IT MEAN TO BE COMPATIBLE?

"Mutual incompatibility was our problem."
"We fell out of love."
"We had irreconcilable differences."
"We just couldn't seem to get along."

These tend to be among the foremost comments made today by people seeking divorce or explaining the demise of a marriage, especially in an era when couples seem prone to divorce for reasons other than adultery, abuse, or abandonment. A recent Gallup Poll confirmed this trend with a startling statistic: some 47 percent of marriages now end with mutual incompatibility as the reason for the dissolution of the relationship.

The sad fact is that the vast majority of people who make these comments once were madly in love with the person from whom they are now estranged. In some cases, they could hardly be pried apart from the spouse—literally and figuratively! The last thing they anticipated was a day when passion would wane, conflicts would become entrenched to the point of silent hatred, or wedded *bliss* would degenerate into a warlike *blitz*.

What makes for mutual compatibility? Or stated another way, can compatibility be defined and recognized? Can people discern in advance of marriage that they will have the ability to *reconcile* their differences? Is there something that couples might do to determine prior to the wedding day that they will be able to get along and succeed in marriage?

This book is based on "yes" answers to these questions. As a starting point for our discussion, let's take a look at what draws people together in the first place.

Why Do People Marry?

Men and women are drawn to each other for a wide variety of reasons—and for a wide variety of relationships. Not all of these relationships end in marriage.

Someone can like a person a great deal, or even love a person passionately, and yet not marry that person—because one chooses not to marry or the decision is mutual. In many dating relationships, the subject of marriage never even comes up!

Geri and Clark dated for nearly two years in high school before they realized that they were "just friends." As much as they enjoyed each other's company, shared many mutual interests, and found themselves laughing at the same jokes and crying at the same movies, they mutually agreed that

WHAT DOES IT MEAN TO BE COMPATIBLE?

neither of them desired to have an intimate relationship with the other, nor did they desire to build a life together. That didn't keep them from going to the senior prom together, but it did keep them from becoming engaged.

Both went on to marry others whom they met in college, and fortunately, their spouses entered into the friendship so that today, Geri and Peter and Clark and Marjorie are all friends. They attend the same church and frequently go out to dinner together.

Not all good and healthy relationships lead to marriage, nor should they. Relationships that do lead to marriage often have one or more of these desires at their root:

○ A desire for companionship or sexual intimacy. People reach a stage or age in their lives when they simply don't want to live alone, make all of their own decisions, face the future alone, eat breakfast alone, or sleep alone.

○ A need for help. Some people recognize, even at an intuitive level, that they can't do it all by themselves in life.

○ A desire for a shared destiny. Some people feel a need for someone who will work alongside them to fulfill a particular mission or destiny they sense for their lives.

Rarely are these root motivations openly acknowledged or discussed. Most of the time, a person will say in a counseling session, "I just *want* to get married," or "I can't imagine living without this person."

At times, one person in the relationship may have one motivation, and the other person another.

Often, the motivations are tangled up with hormones. The sexual attraction between the two people may be so strong that they are virtually incapable of recognizing anything other than a physiological need to be together.

Still, one or more of these root motivations are nearly always present in both parties. A part of determining in advance of marriage whether a relationship is a sound and potentially lasting one involves getting to the motivational root.

Over the years, I have found it helpful to ask couples—or individuals who have come to me seeking advice about marriage—to focus initially on three facets of their relationship: (1) availability, (2) excitability, and (3) compatibility. The three are very different, yet complementary.

Availability Is a Must

A marriage isn't possible unless both parties are fully available to each other.

I'll never forget the day Joanie came to my office with a starry look in her eyes. She had met her dream guy. Jarrod was tall, good-looking, intelligent, and fun to be with. He had a fast-rising career, he owned his own home, and both of them were members of the same denomination. Best of all, according to Joanie, they communicated well. She and Jarrod—who worked in her office building but for a different company—had met often during the last three weeks for lunch at a cafe close to their work. She was amazed at how easily they could talk about all facets of their lives, even deep and sensitive issues. Ah, yes, it was love, destined to be and

WHAT DOES IT MEAN TO BE COMPATIBLE?

to last forever. There was only one hitch. The more we talked, the more I sensed that she and Jarrod were seeing each other only at lunch.

"Do you ever have dinner together?" I asked, half jokingly.

"Oh, no," she replied. "Not yet."

"Why not?" I asked.

"Well," she admitted after some hesitation, "he's presently married."

"Then he's not available," I advised.

"But he's not happy," she replied quickly. "He's thinking about separating from his wife."

"Why hasn't he already separated?" I asked.

"Well," she continued, now much more seriously than at the outset of her gushing monologue, "because there's a child involved."

"He's not available," I repeated. "Find someone who is truly available to you, Joanie—not someone who already has a wife and family."

I wasn't quite prepared for her tears. "But all of the good men are already taken," she cried.

"No," I tried to comfort her, "they aren't all taken. And if they are, you don't want them if it means having them secondhand. Start looking at the guys who aren't married. I'll bet you find a guy who's thinking that all of the best women are already married."

She did, four months later, and a year to the day after we had talked about Jarrod, she married a young man who was single and very well matched to her.

I am continually amazed at the number of stories—in

paperback books, soap operas, prime-time TV shows, and on the big screen—that portray adultery and infidelity as the norm. Let's be very clear about this point in approaching compatibility. A person who is married to someone else or who is seriously involved with another person in anticipation of marriage is *not* available.

Accessible to Each Other

Availability means far more than being unmarried, however. It also means being available in all areas of life—of making oneself vulnerable and accessible to the other person emotionally and materially.

About a year after Sharon was divorced, she began dating. Over the next eighteen months, she seriously dated four men in fairly rapid succession. No one was right for her. Finally, she met Ben and things really clicked into place. Not only did they have lots of the same interests and desires, but in Sharon's words, "He doesn't shut me out of any part of his life."

"Great," I replied in encouragement. "That's important!"

"I didn't realize how important that was until I met Ben," she said. "In my relationship with each of those other guys, we came to a point where a door was closed and a big 'Do Not Enter' sign was put out. There was something with each one of them that just couldn't be discussed or shared. With one it was a hurt in the past and also his relationship with God. With another it was his current relationship with his ex-wife. With the third guy it was his business. With the fourth guy it was his relationship with his parents. I was a bit bowled over by Ben, who was so willing to talk about and

WHAT DOES IT MEAN TO BE COMPATIBLE?

share every part of his life. I kept waiting for the 'No Trespassing' sign to emerge, but it never did."

Time and Presence

For Merline, the issue of availability was not marital, emotional, or physical; it involved time and presence.

Merline had begun corresponding with a soldier in a pen-pal program that her sorority started during Desert Storm. She exchanged countless letters, photos, and phone calls with Frank during the next several years, with an increasing volume and intensity in the past six months. She felt that she knew Frank extremely well, and that they had a great deal in common. In his latest letter, he had asked her to consider marrying him. He had told her that he was going to call soon and was hoping to hear a "yes" answer.

"What do you think?" she asked after she had told me about Frank and their common interests and background.

"How much time have you actually spent together?" I asked.

"I flew to Virginia to meet him for a long weekend just two months ago," she replied. The weekend had been a glorious one, packed with activities. She had spent about an hour with his parents prior to flying home.

"Is that all?" I asked.

"Yes," she said.

"Then my advice," I said, "is to wait in making your decision until you have had some more time to spend with Frank. You only know by phone calls and letters what he wants you to know about him. Wait and see how compatible you are in day-to-day living, working, dating, and decision making." Frank was not yet fully available to Merline in time and presence.

ARE WE COMPATIBLE?

Why is availability so important to a relationship? It is the foundation on which any kind of compatibility is built or recognized. If two people don't spend enough time together, don't communicate about all areas of their lives, or are holding out on each other emotionally, mentally, or spiritually, there is an automatic lessening of their ability to find out how compatible they are or aren't! If a marriage is entered into with only a partial look at or partial experience with each other's opinions, habits, mood swings, feelings, or behavioral quirks, the marriage is based on half-truths. What isn't known about the other person may be the most important thing to know.

Before considering marriage seriously or entering into marriage, make sure each person is fully available to the other. If that isn't the case, ask, Why not? What will it take for both to become fully available? Are both willing to make the effort that it may take to be fully available to each other? If not, why not? If so, when?

Availability is not compatibility, but it is a key to discovering and developing compatibility.

Excitability Involves More Than Sexual Attraction

Psychologists, philosophers, and poets alike have pondered sexual attraction for centuries, and there are still no formulas, axioms, or predictability scales for determining why or how people are attracted to each other. And frankly, I'm not sure there ever should be. One of the great mysteries of life is sexual attraction, and so be it. A life without mystery would be boring.

What Does It Mean to Be Compatible?

The fact is that sexual attraction keeps the human race alive. We may not know the cause of sexual attraction, but we do know its result: babies. Regardless of spiritual beliefs or cultural background, people around the world have a sense that the capacity for sexual activity and the bearing of children is a part of what makes marriage what it is. A marriage without sexual activity is dull, if not void.

If you aren't sexually attracted to or physically excited by your intended spouse, think again. Sexual attraction is part of what makes a marriage fun, meaningful, and fulfilling.

Conversely, the excitability dimension of a marriage relationship should not be exclusively sexual. There are at least four other areas in which you will want to find your beloved one exciting.

Mental

Do you like thinking about your beloved? Do you think about him or her often? Do you anticipate what your beloved might think, say, or do? Do you daydream about being with your beloved in ways that don't involve sex?

A man once said to me about his fiancée, "I think about her all the time."

"What is she doing in your thoughts?" I asked.

"Oh, lots of things," he said. "Cooking dinner in the kitchen of her apartment, cutting flowers in her garden, teaching the four-year-olds at Sunday school, answering the phone at her office, working with an artist on an ad, sitting across the table from me in a restaurant."

"And you like thinking about her in those settings?"

"Oh, yeah," he said. "I want to crawl right into my thoughts and be there with her."

What a delightful word picture!

Conversational

Do you find your beloved to be an interesting conversationalist? Do you find her opinions and ideas interesting? Do you enjoy hearing the news of his day? Do you anticipate eagerly the next time you can get together and talk over what is happening in both of your lives? Do you like talking about the future together? Do you long to know all the details of your beloved's past?

Much of any long-standing relationship is built by talking. If a conversational relationship doesn't include elements of excitement, you are far less likely to talk to each other. When you talk less, you obviously have less opportunity for communicating. When communication breaks down, so do other areas of a relationship.

Visual

Do you enjoy watching your beloved? Do you like the way your beloved moves, laughs, walks, talks, and gestures?

The traditional viewpoint has been that men are much more visually attracted to women than women are to men. I haven't found that to be the case in the young people with whom I have conversed or counseled. Men are women watchers, and women are men watchers. Part of the initial attraction between men and women nearly always is based on visual cues.

What Does It Mean to Be Compatible?

Accomplishments

Do you get excited about what your beloved is doing and accomplishing in life? Do you take pleasure in the successes? Do you value and appreciate the goals being sought?

Lisa showed vocal excitement for her husband, Craig, who was a baseball player in the minor leagues. She genuinely enjoyed going to his games and rooting for the home team with all her might. She was excited about Craig's batting average and his career and potential to be a major-league player. And in turn, she was excited about Craig!

Excitability includes being excited about your beloved's potential and the accomplishments in pursuit of that potential.

Why is excitability important to compatibility? Because it compels people continually to search for greater commonality and ways to bridge differences. If availability is the foundation on which compatibility is built, excitability keeps a person building.

Compatibility Makes for Endurance

Both availability and excitability are important for a relationship to endure, grow, and be fulfilling to both parties in a marriage. But compatibility is vital.

There are moments in any relationship in which one or the other person cannot be fully available to the other—mentally, emotionally, physically, or in the practical dimensions of time and space. There are also moments in any relationship in which excitement wanes or is diminished, perhaps because of the stresses of life or changing circumstances. If two people have a high degree of compatibility, however, they nearly always are able to ride out those times of less availability or diminished passion. Their compatibility, in fact, pushes them toward making themselves more available to each other or toward rekindling the excitement of their relationship.

So, a marriage can exist without constant availability or intense excitability. But it has little chance of enduring and being fulfilling without a high degree of ongoing compatibility.

The Ability to "Get Along Well"

I remember vividly the first time I heard the term *compatibility*. I was with my grandparents, sitting in their car on the main street of our small town.

In his later years of retirement, Grandpa enjoyed driving uptown in the afternoons, parking the car along the main street, and watching the people walk by. If someone stopped to chat and share a little gossip, or if a friend walked by and invited him to have a soda at the drugstore, so much the better. Whenever possible, Grandma joined him. On this occasion, my brother and I had been privileged to go along.

Grandma or Grandpa had a comment to make concerning just about every person who walked by. The response to one couple was, in Grandma's voice, "They're so compatible."

I was about seven at the time—an age when new words are curiosities—so I asked, "What's that mean?"

Grandma replied, "It means that they get along together real well."

What Does It Mean to Be Compatible?

"Are you and Grandpa compatible?" I asked, eager to try out the new word.

"Oh, yes," Grandma replied. "We're very compatible." When I looked at Grandpa, he just winked, and then he smiled and reached over to take Grandma's hand. That moment is one of my fondest memories of my grandparents. Instinctively, I knew that compatibility was "good" and that every couple should have what Grandpa and Grandma had in their relationship. Only years later did I realize that "getting along together real well" was not always the case between spouses.

Grandma's definition of compatibility is still one of the best I know. "Getting along together real well" implies that partners have a lot in common and that they relate to each other with mutuality and ease. It also has an element of time to it. Part of getting along together is a learning process—a compatibility achieved over time.

For purposes of more precise definition, discussion, and direction setting, however, we probably need a slightly more sophisticated definition of compatibility than that offered by my grandmother. Compatibility, for our purposes in this book, is defined as follows: *Compatibility is the capacity for harmony and agreement that leads to a consistent way to live.*

Let's take a closer look at this definition.

Chapter 2

A COMPATIBILITY MODEL

Each person in a marriage relationship brings the past, present, and potential for the future. Each person brings foibles and quirks, as well as aptitudes, talents, and sterling qualities. It's not enough to be compatible in one area or two areas. Compatibility refers to *all* of each person in the relationship.

A long-standing biblical definition of marriage is that "the two become one flesh." This oneness does not refer to a sexual bond alone; in all fleshly ways—from daily schedules to family budgets to dinner plans—the two function as one.

In becoming a couple, of course, the two people do not actually melt together to become one person. Rather, the two must find a way of fitting together so that like two pieces of a puzzle, they are locked in a relationship so tightly that they are as one piece.

ARE WE COMPATIBLE?

Fifty-Fifty?

Some people advocate a fifty-fifty approach to marriage. They seem to envision two people in marriage as being something of a mirror image of each other—identical halves that come together to create a perfect circle. Some contend that opposites attract. Others regard a good marriage as one in which the two people are very much alike in all ways.

Neither, in my opinion, is a realistic approach to the way people are and the way a marriage functions. I have yet to see a lasting, fulfilling marriage in which the two people are true opposites. Opposite personalities, opposing points of view, different backgrounds, dissimilar goals, and unshared interests do not lead to harmony.

But I haven't seen a good marriage in which the two people are cookie-cutter images of each other, either. In the first place, no two people have exactly the same backgrounds, interests, opinions, goals, emotional temperament, and personality. If a couple portrays itself as such, one person has completely sublimated his or her identity. One person is dominant to the point of total dominance, and the other is subordinate to the point of nonexistence. That is not a good marriage, although it may be a fine example of a dictatorship.

Ninety-Ten?

Some people speak of marriage as being a ninety-ten proposition—each person giving 90 percent all of the time and expecting only 10 percent in return.

This model refers to effort, not mutuality. Trying hard and

A Compatibility Model

giving more are not synonymous with commonality. In discussing compatibility, we are concerned ultimately with the willingness of each person to give to the other and sustain the relationship, but we are concerned primarily with the *capacity* for that relationship to exist in the first place. We are looking first and foremost at similarities and mutualities based on what is already inherent in each person, not on the effort each person is going to make to keep the marriage alive and well.

Overlapping?

Other counselors have pictured marriage as an overlapping of interests, with the perfect marriage being the one that has a complete overlap. This image is a functional one as far as I am concerned, but I am troubled by the tendency to think that the "extra" pieces that don't overlap should in some way be cut off, trimmed away, or dismissed. The areas in which one doesn't overlap with the other tend to be problematic.

The Jagged Pieces Model

The model we are using in this book is based on an understanding of the persons in the relationship looking something like the "Compatibility Model."

Note several things about this model. Each piece has its own identity—its own shape. Though roughly the same size, the shape of each piece is unique. Each piece has a ragged edge. There is an obvious area in which the two pieces appear that they will fit together, and there are areas that don't match up.

ARE WE COMPATIBLE?

These pieces are not unlike us human beings. Each of us has rough spots, sharp points, dull cavities, and jagged edges that make us distinctly who we are. When you come together with another person in what you hope will be a "locked together" relationship, you are looking for ways in which you and your beloved might fit together. Furthermore, you are looking for as many ways as possible to fit with the other person.

COMPATIBILITY MODEL A

Earlier we talked about the issue of availability. As much as you try to be available, there are areas of your life that you are not capable of sharing with another person or that the other person doesn't care anything about.

Sandi, for example, is an avid tennis player. Her husband,

A COMPATIBILITY MODEL

Rod, is a couch potato. His idea of sport is taking a rod and reel out to a local pond and sitting there for several hours in solitude. He rarely catches a fish. It could be because he rarely baits his hook! There's very little about Sandi's tennis life that interests Rod and very little about Rod's fishing excursions that excites Sandi. On Saturday mornings, the two go their separate ways, and they rarely discuss what they do on Saturday mornings. The hobby area of their individual lives is not an integral facet of their marriage.

That does not mean they are unavailable to each other in the strictest sense. Should Rod need Sandi to accompany him on a Saturday morning, she would be willing to do so. When Sandi plays in the annual club tournament, she values Rod's attendance, and he dutifully goes and applauds at the appropriate times.

Both parties in the marriage are equally committed to defining certain areas of their lives as being unimportant or unnecessary to their life as a married couple. The situation would be quite different if Rod was eager to hear how Sandi's backhand was working on the court.

The first challenge a couple faces in compatibility is in defining the overall "capacity" of the relationship—essentially defining what is in and what is out.

Three elements need to be kept in a marriage relationship: (1) people, (2) feelings, and (3) plans.

Keeping People Inside the Marriage

Vern and Lil made a big mistake early in their marriage when both chose to keep relationships separate from their marriage. For Vern, it was his ongoing relationship with his first wife, Valerie. For Lil, it was her relationship with her father. It took only a few months for Lil to begin to resent the presence of another woman in Vern's life, especially the time he spent solving her problems or meeting her needs. Vern, in turn, resented the fact that Lil turned constantly to her father for advice rather than to him.

Only when Vern and Lil made Valerie and Dad "on limits" to their marriage did they begin to find ways of working through their individual resentments. Eventually, Valerie was completely eliminated from their relationship by mutual consent. Dad was consulted far less, and only when Vern and Lil consulted him together.

People need to be kept inside the marriage relationship in virtually all cases. As soon as a person is made exclusive to one partner, the opportunity exists for jealousy and misunderstanding.

Keeping Feelings Inside the Marriage

Feelings need to be kept within a relationship. When a person says, "I don't want you around when I cry," or "I don't ever want to see you cry," a part of the person's identity is eliminated from the relationship. The same holds true for any expression of emotion.

You should be able to express what you feel in the presence of your spouse. If the other person is uncomfortable with your expression of feelings, or believes that your feelings are expressed too often or too deeply, compromise and negotiation may be necessary. But completely denying the expression of feeling opens the door to sublimation and resulting self-denial. Both lead to bitterness, an emotion that is a marriage destroyer.

A COMPATIBILITY MODEL

Sharing Plans in the Marriage

When one person in a marriage makes plans that exclude the other person or that are kept secret, the marriage is immediately in trouble. In essence, one person is preparing to move in a direction without consulting, advising, or discussing the move with the other person.

Plans include meetings, parties, goals, aspirations, and financial dealings. Time and again, counselors hear this lament from a person who has been left or rejected in a marriage: "I didn't have a clue as to what was going on!"

The fact is, the person wasn't given a clue. In many cases, the person is the victim of a secret plan that the other person was forging in the mind or in reality for some time.

Keep all of your plans open and above board within the marriage.

In defining the capacity of a marriage, we are ultimately defining all of the ways in which the two people are going to expect to relate to each other. Once these broad areas are defined, we look for ways in which the two lives might fit together.

Going back to our definition of compatibility, we find the phrase "capacity for harmony." Harmony is the "fit together" we are seeking.

The Capacity for Harmony: Looking for a Good Fit

Compatibility in marriage is based on finding a way to hook your life and your beloved's life together.

ARE WE COMPATIBLE?

You are looking for harmony, not equality—at least not equality in the purest meaning of the word. You should *not* expect every aspect of your nature to fit perfectly with a corresponding facet of the other person. The best you can hope for, realistically, is a good fit. You and your beloved need to find as many points of natural harmony as possible.

As part of my music education in high school, I took a simple course in harmony. In studying chords, I quickly noted that good harmonies were nearly always based on thirds, fourths, fifths, and octaves—in other words, every two notes in a chord were three, four, five, or eight tones apart. Those sounds are the most harmonious to the Western ear.

A "third" chord is not necessarily more harmonious to the ear than a chord based on a "fourth" or an "octave." The notes are simply farther apart or closer together. The sense of harmony remains. What is important is the progression from one chord to the next.

How does this relate to people and relationships?

First, compatibility is not a matter of how close two people are. Some couples can spend twenty-four hours a day together, every day of every year for a decade, and be happy as clams. Other couples can see each other one week out of four and be equally happy; spending all their time together would probably destroy the marriage.

The amount of time two people spend in each other's presence does not necessarily make for harmony. Neither is the amount of talking they do.

Some couples seem to discuss every aspect of their relationship and lives on a nonstop basis. Other couples are virtually mute by comparison. Still other couples reaffirm their love for each other perhaps once a year, or maybe once a lifetime, and they will readily tell you that they see no point in overstating their obvious commitment to each other.

Closeness in communication is not necessarily a prerequisite for harmony. And to the surprise of some, neither is frequent sexual activity.

Some couples have a great deal of sexual activity in their marriages. They can't seem to get enough of each other, and they take great pleasure in their physical closeness. Other couples delight in sexual activity only two or three times a month, and they claim that more frequent contact makes their sexual life less meaningful. The frequency of sexual activity that a couple enjoys is not necessarily a prerequisite for harmony.

So, what is important to harmony? *The existence of many parallels within the relationship.*

No marriage can be completely, naturally harmonious. Some of the pieces in any relationship inevitably will be out of sync. One person zigs where the other zags. Gaps widen or narrow without an even pattern.

A part of compatibility is finding a way to make the unmatched pieces conform to the whole. This takes agreement and an ability to bridge gaps.

Returning to our definition of compatibility, we find the phrase "capacity for . . . agreement." In areas in which two people don't have natural harmony, they need to find a way to reach agreement. Agreement may take various forms and it may be derived by various means, but it must be forged for the two people truly to be linked together in a way that is tight enough for them to function as one entity.

ARE WE COMPATIBLE?

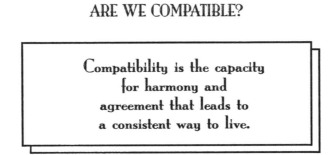

Compatibility is the capacity
for harmony and
agreement that leads to
a consistent way to live.

Let's take another look at the model of compatibility that is at the core of what we will do in the following pages.

COMPATIBILITY MODEL B

The two pieces have jagged areas that are parallel. Other areas are not parallel. These areas, however, are bridged. The result, for all practical purposes, is that the areas are linked in a way allowing the whole of the two pieces to move together

A COMPATIBILITY MODEL

as if they were one piece. The fit may not be natural, but it is a fit. An artificial way of bridging the gap has brought the two sides together.

Is a bridge any less effective than close harmony? Not really.

Consider a river that has formed a deep gorge, the two sides of which are parallel and close enough together for a person to cross from one side to the next with a flying leap and the help of a rope hanging from a tall tree. Consider that same river flowing wide across a prairie. A bridge spans it at one point. In both cases, people have the means of getting from one side to the next. The same holds true in a relationship.

There are areas in which the partners naturally get along. They rarely have to discuss these areas of their lives. In other areas, they need to negotiate, compromise, accommodate, or find ways of working out a difference in a way that brings satisfaction to each person. This bridge in their relationship is something they have had to work at, through communication and trial and error, and sometimes over a fairly long period of time. The result, however, is a way to live that becomes predictable and consistent, and bears all the hallmarks of agreement evident in the naturally harmonious areas. An agreement gives consistency and strength to the relationship in an area where it was previously inconsistent (unparalleled) and, thus, weak.

Compatibility is nearly always a blend of natural harmony and achieved agreement. The good news is that you can learn to be compatible with another person, even if you and your beloved are not naturally compatible.

ARE WE COMPATIBLE?

Compatibility and Consistency

Note the final phrase of our compatibility definition: "the capacity for harmony and agreement that *leads to a consistent way to live.*"

What is the value of consistency? Consistency implies that the two partners of a marriage are capable of responding to life spontaneously and naturally as one entity. That's the goal of nearly all marriages. That's the oneness most people crave. That's the manifestation of a good marriage that most people desire.

Consistency also implies that the "lumps" of marriage have been worked out to the point that the batter of the relationship is smooth. Each person understands the rules of the marriage. Each knows where he or she stands. Each knows what is expected. Each has a sense of what is required. And in turn, each has a sense of duty, responsibility, and role. In turn, each person is able to do and be all each is capable of being within the marriage. And when that happens, joy and fulfillment result.

Consistency doesn't happen quickly. It takes time and effort. But compatibility makes possible the harmony and agreement that can lead to consistency.

I once overheard an older woman describe herself and her husband to a third party. "We're just a couple of old shoes," she said, and then she added with a little chuckle, "but I guess the good part is that we've been walking down the same road and we're worn out about evenly."

Compatibility makes for endurance.

A Compatibility Model

A Balanced Approach

Let me remind you again that the premise of this book is *not* that compatibility is the sole ingredient of a good marriage—one that lasts, is fulfilling to both parties, and provides deep inner joy. Availability and excitability are also ingredients that need to be nurtured and maintained. However, compatibility is the mainstay of a solid relationship. Without it, a relationship withers.

The most important questions to ask, then, in preparing for marriage are ones that directly relate to compatibility. In the coming chapters, you'll encounter five main areas of compatibility that are vital to a marriage: (1) physical compatibility, (2) compatibility of background, (3) emotional compatibility, (4) compatibility of goals and dreams, and (5) compatibility of values. In each area, you'll be given a chance to take a self-test—with test forms for you and your beloved to complete—and then to evaluate the degree of compatibility.

Don't be discouraged if you and your beloved are less than harmonious in one area. There's still the possibility of forging agreements in that dimension. If you and your beloved are incompatible to a great extent in three or more areas, however, you probably need to rethink your plans for marriage.

Above all, work your way through all five areas of compatibility. Don't draw conclusions too quickly or too easily. Be honest with yourself in expressing your opinions and in facing your relationship.

ARE WE COMPATIBLE?

Overcoming the Fear Factor

Some people who are "in love" and planning to be married prefer to ignore certain patterns in the relationship. Some don't want to talk about the relationship or potential areas of conflict. It's almost as if they believe, *If we talk about it, it will come to pass.*

The exact opposite is true. The differences are already there. They will manifest themselves sooner or later. Even if you don't talk about your differences now, you will face the consequences of them.

Others are afraid that if they talk about the relationship, they will destroy it. Some of the magic and mystery will evaporate. Cold logic will replace the warmth of their feelings.

The truth is that feelings are temporal. They come and go in waves, even in the best of marriages. Passion ebbs and flows. Some of the magic and mystery of the engagement period does evaporate once a couple marry. Is it better that this mysterious aura lifts prior to the reciting of marriage vows or after the ceremony?

I contend that it's better for a couple to have a look at the reality of their life together before the wedding ceremony. That does not mean love will lessen. The odds are fairly equal that love will intensify. As new discoveries are made about each other, the likelihood is good that the discoveries will be wonderful ones. And if a truth is revealed that is truly damaging to the relationship, how much better that it is revealed prior to the wedding than after!

A Compatibility Model

The real fear of most people in facing premarital discussions about the relationship is that the relationship will end. The wedding won't happen; the marriage won't take place.

That does happen, but not often. The more common result is that the two people have a much clearer understanding of potential pitfalls and are thus able to steer their way through them or around them. They are better equipped to cope with problems that do arise.

In cases where weddings are called off, both parties nearly always rejoice in that fact after a few days, weeks, or months. Rarely is the emotional pain devastating or long-lived. Rather, there is a sense of relief at avoiding a tragedy. And there nearly always is a strong conviction that someone more suitable is out there.

Have courage, and forge ahead. In exploring these five areas of compatibility, do so with the hope that you will be finding a way of strengthening your relationship, not damaging it. This book takes the stance of being 100 percent pro marriage and 200 percent pro *good* marriage.

Ultimately, most people want a good marriage. A good marriage is probably the greatest blessing a person can experience in life. And all good marriages have one thing in common: a high degree of compatibility.

Chapter 3

Physical Compatibility I: Sexual Compatibility

In today's world, virginity at the time of one's marriage may be less common than it once was, but it is also more common than many people seem to think. The certain fact is that most young people—even though they may not have experienced sexual intercourse—have a considerable number of sexual experiences prior to entering marriage. Physical expressions such as holding hands or kissing or embracing are a part of the sexual experience continuum.

I know of only one couple who did not engage in this kind of behavior prior to their engagement to be married. Carey was brought up in a very disciplined and religious home. She was admonished not to kiss a boy unless she was sure he was the one she was going to marry. And that's precisely the path she followed. By the time she met Tom, she was sweet twenty-three and had never been kissed.

ARE WE COMPATIBLE?

"You're kidding," I said when she first told me her story over coffee one afternoon.

"No," she assured me, "that's the way it was. Mother always said that I needed to be sure that the guy really loved me for who I was, not how I kissed, and I took her advice. Tom and I dated for five months. In fact, we saw each other almost every day. We became quite close."

"And never kissed?" I still could hardly believe it.

"No. We did hold hands, though. But not in public."

"You're making this up," I said.

"No, really. Tom proposed to me, and then he asked my father for my hand in marriage, and *then* we kissed."

"And?"

"And, it was so good we haven't stopped kissing!" she laughed. Tom and Carey have been married now for twenty-four years, and they have a strong, joyful marriage.

Past Issues Linked to Sexual Compatibility

Ghosts in the bedroom—present in the thoughts and images that one partner in the marriage may have about another person with whom he or she has had some form of sexual contact—are a problem for many young people today. They are probably the foremost reason to stay celibate until marriage and then to remain faithful in marriage, but they are rarely talked about.

Approach the issue of sexual compatibility through frank discussions about each person's sexual past. You don't need to know each intimate detail, but you can and should ask questions such as these:

PHYSICAL COMPATIBILITY I

○ Is there someone in the past that you still think about in terms of a physical relationship you had, or wish you had experienced?

○ Do you compare me often to anybody else physically or sexually?

○ Do you feel guilty about your physical or sexual behavior with any person with whom you have had a relationship in the past?

A "yes" answer to any of these questions can present a problem in your relationship.

It's nearly impossible for a person to compete with a fantasy or a memory. Fantasies are always bigger and better than real life; sugarcoated memories are always sweeter than present reality. Guilt, too, is a burden that tends to be transferred from one relationship to the next. Fantasies, memories, and guilt need to be cleansed from a relationship before true sexual compatibility can be established.

Another important question is very difficult for most young people to ask each other:

○ Have you had sexual intercourse with another person?

I have found that a surprising number of people don't want to know the answer to this question. They want to believe that they are the "first and only" in the person's life.

If one person has had sexual intercourse and the other hasn't, there's an immediate sense of imbalance. Forgiveness needs to take place—forgiveness of the person by the one who is still a virgin, and self-forgiveness by the one who has violated the purity expected.

"But," you may say, "what about the person who wants to marry somebody more experienced?"

I've heard that line for years, but in all of my counseling and conversational hours spent with young men and women, I've never encountered one person who truly wants to marry someone more experienced. Young men and women want to marry virgins who have waited for them.

If both persons have had sexual experiences in the past, there needs to be mutual forgiveness and some line of demarcation made between the past and now.

If both persons are virgins, both need to be advised what not to expect and to be encouraged to laugh a lot as they explore a brand-new world.

Cleansing the Past

One of the most traditional prayers in the history of the Christian church has been, "Cleanse the thoughts of our hearts by the inspiration of Your Holy Spirit." Part of that cleansing process for many young people with past sexual encounters is an opportunity to enter a defined period of celibacy and purity prior to entering into a new sexual relationship within the bounds of marriage. You may want to consider that possibility.

A defined period of celibacy marks a clear transitional period in the individual's life and the life of the relationship. As one man told me who had lived a celibate life for a full year prior to his marriage, "The most important thing was that *I* felt cleansed going into our marriage. I felt as if I was bringing to my bride a me that I had never brought to anyone else."

PHYSICAL COMPATIBILITY I

I asked the young woman how she felt, having entered her marriage as a virgin even though she knew her husband had a long list of prior sex partners. She said, "Without that time of cleansing and abstinence on his part, I don't think I could have married him. But when I saw that he was willing to discipline himself in that way—and for a full year—I found my respect for him growing and my hurt feelings about his past fading away.

Five Signs to Heed

Apart from asking about a person's sexual past and finding a way of resolving it, five signs tend to predict certain aspects of sexual compatibility.

1. A Desire to Touch

The desire to touch—to want to hold hands, embrace, walk with arms around each other, kiss, and snuggle—is natural for young people who are sexually attracted to each other. The real question to ask is, Is either uncomfortable with the touches of the other person?

Maryanne loved to touch and be touched, but she felt touching was appropriate only in private. Her fiancé, Jim, didn't care where they were. The conflict was a matter not of desire but of perceived appropriateness. Maryanne and Jim were actually compatible in this area, but only when they agreed to keep their touching out of the public eye.

Ask yourself, Does my beloved rebuff my advances? If so, do I know why? Do I feel uncomfortable with my beloved's touching? Talk about your answers to these questions to find out if the issues are a matter of propriety, inexperience, or a true difference in desires to be touched and to touch.

ARE WE COMPATIBLE?

2. *A Comfortable Silence*

You and your beloved need to be comfortable in each other's presence, regardless of situations, circumstances, or noise.

Ask yourselves, Are we both comfortable when silence falls between us? Is each able to relax fully in the other's presence without a constant stream of chatter? Does either of us feel a need to analyze every action or discuss every act in our relationship?

Cindy is a talker. Jeff doesn't talk much to anyone about anything. He initially found Cindy's nonstop chatter both amusing and interesting. After a while, Cindy was annoyed by Jeff's silence. She came to the point of believing, "He never talks to me!" Jeff, on the other hand, found that he needed space.

In counseling, they realized that they had vastly different needs for input and communication. That was especially true for intimate moments. Cindy needed verbal reassurance that Jeff was satisfied, happy, pleased. Jeff needed to relax in silence.

Jeff and Cindy married—in other areas of their lives they were very compatible—but they had a hard time adjusting in this area of silence and intimacy. Cindy gradually came to see that Jeff's silence should be interpreted as pleasure and satisfaction. Jeff, in turn, made more of an effort to tell Cindy how he felt. They forged an agreement where natural harmony didn't exist.

If you feel uneasy in the silence of your beloved, if you wish for more silence, or if you deeply desire more feedback, find some way to talk about this together. It may be a difficult conversation, especially since the tendency of at least one of you appears to be not to want to talk. But it's an important conversation to have. A different tolerance for or desire for silence can greatly affect your relationship, particularly in intimate moments.

3. A Willingness to Stop

Passion, contrary to what some young people seem to think, is subject to the will. These two rules govern passion: (1) don't say no or stop unless you mean it, and (2) if your beloved says no or stop, believe him or her.

If your beloved crosses the "no" or "stop" message, be extremely wary of entering into a long-term relationship with this person.

Ask yourself, too, What other areas of life is this person unlikely to be able to control?

Also be wary if neither seems willing or able to say no to passionate desire. Unbridled passion truly does tend to run wild, often beyond the bounds of marriage.

4. A Willingness to Talk About Sexual Behaviors

Can the two of you talk freely and openly about your sexual activity? If you don't like the way your beloved has just kissed you, do you say so? If you resent the stilted silence that seems to envelop both of you after you have said no, can you talk about it? If you feel rebuffed or rejected, can you talk to your beloved about it?

Most people are reluctant initially to talk about sexual behaviors they don't like. It's easier for most to begin conversations about sexual activity with what they do like.

Emphasize what you enjoy. Then you can proceed to what you don't enjoy.

Each couple ultimately discovers what works best for both partners and what is most enjoyable. They tend to find out through trial and error, and through conversations. The faster way to the greatest pleasure is through conversation!

Be wary if your beloved doesn't want to talk at all about sex. Find out why not.

For Wayne, talking about any sexual behavior with Laura was nearly impossible, even though they had been engaged for eight months and were about to be married. He discovered in their marriage counseling with their pastor that Laura was very inexperienced sexually (having never even held hands with a boy prior to Wayne), and that she had virtually no understanding of the biological and physiological aspects of sex. Laura's unwillingness to talk about sex was a combination of her shyness and a tremendous lack of knowledge. Once she became informed—which happily occurred prior to her wedding night!—she was much more willing to talk about sexual behaviors with Wayne.

She commented several years after their wedding, "When someone finally explained sex to me, I felt as if a light came on inside me. Most of the things I was feeling with Wayne were new to me and a great mystery. I needed the assurance that it was OK for me to like and respond to certain ways he touched me and kissed me."

If your beloved won't talk about sexual behaviors and your shared sexual activity with you, find out why not. It may be a matter of ignorance or shyness. Or it may be something much more problematic.

5. A Natural Ease in Coupling

Some couples naturally seem to fit together. Their hands feel right together. Each likes the way the other kisses, intuitively and instinctively. They easily embrace and are very comfortable being close to each other. When they walk together, they naturally fall into step with each other.

This natural ease is generally harmonious compatibility at work. It's usually marked by lighthearted humor and mutual flirtatious teasing. (It's tough to laugh at yourselves when you are working at something.)

This is not to say that couples can't learn to "couple" with greater ease, or that natural coupling occurs instantly or not at all. Most couples tend to grow together.

Note whether you are at ease with each other physically, and if not, find ways to enhance your ease. In this case, you probably don't need to talk about the matter as much as you need to observe how the other person moves, and find ways of adapting and responding appropriately.

If, however, it seems that no matter what you do, you always seem to be out of sync with each other physically—and both of you desire to be in sync—get help from a trustworthy third party.

Honestly Confronting Sexual Orientation

From your discussions about past sexual activity and your observations of the five signs, you can probably draw accurate conclusions about the degree to which you and your beloved will be naturally compatible sexually.

One area that we haven't discussed needs to be addressed

in a straightforward manner. If you question whether your beloved is homosexual, find out if your doubts or suspicions are grounded in reality. Don't wonder or worry about it. Get answers.

There's no bypassing an honest, frank discussion about this matter. Don't leap to conclusions, which may be false. Don't talk yourself out of your concerns; they may be valid.

If you realize you are thinking about your beloved one, *He doesn't respond like any other boy I've ever dated,* or *She doesn't seem to react to me the way any other girl has,* take note.

Fidelity Is Crucial to Marital Trust

In exploring sexual compatibility, ask yourself the ultimate question of importance: Will this person be faithful to me?

Fidelity is crucial to a good marriage. Loyalty is vital. If fidelity and loyalty are breached, the ability to trust is wounded, nearly always severely and often mortally. A marriage without trust isn't a marriage.

How can you tell if a person will be faithful to you? Honestly appraise whether he or she is faithful to you now. Does the person continually flirt with others? Have you caught the person cheating on you, lying to you about involvement with others, or insisting that you "give more space" to permit relationships with others apart from you?

Fidelity is the ability to bond to one person and remain faithful to that person without regard to circumstances or the passing of time. The only way to pretest fidelity is to spend enough time together so that you and your beloved experience adverse circumstances! Four of the most obvious circumstances that test fidelity are (1) disagreements, (2) distance, (3) disasters, and (4) delightful temptations.

1. Disagreements

What happens when you fight? Does your beloved immediately seek solace in the arms of someone else? Be wary if that happens. Arguments and disagreements are inevitable in marriage.

2. Distance

Fidelity is always put to the test when you are apart. What happens when one of you leaves town? Can you trust your beloved to be content waiting for you if you are away overnight or over the summer, or have to travel overseas? If you are anticipating a career that involves significant amounts of travel, can you trust your beloved to be faithful to you while you are apart?

3. Disasters

Sickness, natural catastrophe, or human-created havoc can cause some people to want to run away and hide. The person who runs away very often finds open and waiting arms. How do you and your beloved respond to tough times and difficult circumstances? Do you turn to each other for comfort, advice, and strength, or do you turn to others?

4. Delightful Temptations

What happens when you are at a gathering together? Are you left alone while your beloved one flirts with every other person in the room?

ARE WE COMPATIBLE?

The Impact of Abuse on Sexual Compatibility

Although nobody likes to face the fact that a loved one may have been abused as a child, the estimate today among sexual-abuse researchers is that as many as one in four young women has experienced some form of abuse in her life—verbal, physical, or sexual.

These experiences can greatly affect the sexual relationship of a couple, especially so, it seems, if the prior abuse has not been openly acknowledged and some form of healing therapy received.

Keith's fiancée, Christine, was satisfied with far less physical contact than he desired. She was uncommunicative about sex and yet eager to do "whatever you want." He said in a conversation with me, "It's like she'd go limp in my arms. Her attitude was one of 'do whatever you want and wake me when you're through.' All I was doing was kissing her, nothing more. I couldn't help thinking, *I wonder if she could stay awake during sex.*"

I asked Keith if they had ever discussed Christine's past sexual experiences, and he admitted that when he had asked her about former relationships, she had clammed up and said she thought it was better to leave the past in the past. I suggested that Christine see a counselor before they made any commitment to be married.

Christine did see a counselor, and after several sessions with him, she began to relay experiences of childhood sexual abuse by an older cousin. Keith stood by Christine during her months of therapy, and eventually, they married.

Females are not alone in being the recipients of abuse. Young males are also physically, verbally, and sexually abused.

PHYSICAL COMPATIBILITY I

The issue is ultimately one of power. When sex or physical contact is associated with expressions of power, the problems are only exaggerated.

Observe your beloved in power-play situations and ask, Does he or she cringe or too easily submit when confronted by another person, regardless of motive or purpose of the assault? Does my beloved respond to power with anger, outbursts, or a power surge? Does my beloved respond to frustration by yelling, displaying anger physically (hitting, slapping, throwing things), or seeking to run away and hide? These are typical responses of people who have been abused. There's help for the victim of abuse, but if the abuse of the past has not been dealt with in a constructive way, the abused person may very well manifest abusive or aberrant behavior within the marriage.

Physical Problems Can Affect Intimacy

Physical problems can manifest themselves in a number of ways, including impotency, frigidity, premature ejaculation, lethargy, an overactive libido, and pain. A high percentage of anorexia and bulimia problems are related to abuse and low self-esteem. If you or your beloved one experiences these problems frequently or routinely, see a physician!

Compatibility in Health, Fitness, and Hygiene

Health, fitness, and hygiene are three issues that affect sexual compatibility, but they also stand on their own as a dimension of general physical compatibility.

ARE WE COMPATIBLE?

If one partner in a marriage is unhealthy, unfit, or unclean, the chances of the couple having a satisfying sex life are slim to none. The ill or unfit marriage partner won't have the energy or desire to engage in intimacy. If cleanliness or unkempt appearance is the problem, the observant partner is likely to be disinterested in intimacy.

On the other hand, a fulfilling sex life is nearly always possible for spouses who are healthy and physically fit, and who make an effort to be as attractive as possible, including being clean.

Health Has a Prominent Role

Apart from sex, health is a major factor in the longevity of any relationship. It may not be a critical factor at the outset of a relationship, unless one or both partners have a physical disability, a chronic physical condition, or a lingering or progressive disease. But over the years, poor health patterns can drain the physical, material, financial, and social vitality of a marriage.

There are several issues to consider.

A Desire for Health

Some people don't care whether they are sick or well. Be wary in considering marriage to such a person. Not only will the person do little to help you stay healthy, but he or she will do little to make sure that your children are born into and nurtured in a healthy environment.

If an agreement is not reached about health issues and good health practices, resentment on the part of one person nearly always erupts. Young lovers tend to think they are going to live forever, and they want the loved one to live that long as well. Anything that threatens longevity or vitality is regarded as an enemy—including health issues—when recognized as a potential threat.

Has your beloved asked you to do something or to consider taking a particular action toward your better health? Listen to him or her. The advice is in your best interest.

Healthy Habits

Some people are concerned about health but do little to promote it in themselves or others. They may not know about good health habits or what is required for adequate nutrition. Or they may lack the will to follow through.

Ask yourself, What does my beloved choose to eat? In what ways does my beloved register a concern for taking care of himself or herself physically? Does my beloved get enough rest and take adequate time for recreational activities?

Observe the habits of your beloved's family. What were the eating and sleeping patterns of your beloved's childhood? Did your beloved receive adequate medical attention as a child and teenager? The habits of childhood very often manifest themselves within a marriage, especially when children are born.

Addictions

Most important, be aware of any addictions of your beloved. Does he or she smoke? Chew tobacco? Drink excessive amounts of alcohol? Go on food binges (especially with sugar-laden or high-fat-content foods)? Is your beloved one perpetually on a diet? Does he or she use illegal substances or rely on uppers and downers to get through life?

ARE WE COMPATIBLE?

Addictions are dangerous to any relationship. They easily lead to abusive dominance or unhealthy emotional reliance.

Also be aware of excesses—for example, bouts of too much drinking, too vigorous an exercise regimen, too stringent a diet. These excesses can lead to addiction or be signs of underlying emotional stress or psychological distress.

Amy, a nondrinker, never questioned Joe's "drinking with the boys" during the months that they dated. She never even registered a complaint when he sometimes called her after midnight in a drunken state. Joe assumed that Amy didn't care that he drank. The truth, however, was that Amy cared a great deal. She simply thought that she could keep Joe from drinking once they were married. She was wrong. Joe had an addiction to alcohol and Amy's pleadings and nagging in the months and years following their wedding only irritated him to the point of drinking more. Fortunately, Joe's employer initiated an intervention that put Joe into a program and affiliation with Alcoholics Anonymous. Amy and Joe are still married, but the scars of alcohol on their relationship are deep and they still face a significant amount of struggle and healing as they find a new way of relating to each other "this side of sobriety."

Paul initially was pleased that Trisha wanted to keep herself a trim size eight. Paul didn't know that Trisha forced herself to maintain her thin appearance. When Trisha nearly died as a result of malnutrition (and physician-diagnosed anorexia nervosa), Paul recognized that Trisha had a problem, and that he loved her so much that he truly didn't care how much she weighed as long as she was alive and healthy. Trisha now weighs nearly thirty pounds more than she did when she first met Paul, but she's healthy, and both are happy.

Chronic Health Problems

If you or your future spouse has a chronic health problem, you need to disclose it *prior to your marriage*. It might range from a serious disease (such as diabetes) to a minor disability (such as dyslexia) to an incurable ailment (such as herpes).

Don't keep secrets regarding your health status or a condition that requires periodic health checkups or ongoing medication, or that might result in your partner being affected.

Fitness Is More than Exercise

Physical fitness implies muscle strength, cardiovascular health, flexibility, and quickness of physical response. Fitness involves far more than exercise. Rather, it is the capacity to engage in normal amounts of physical activity without strain, injury, or fatigue.

Exercise can lead to greater levels of fitness, of course, but adequate amounts of sleep and good nutrition are also required for a person to be fit.

Fitness tends to affect a relationship in two broad ways: stamina and laziness.

Stamina is the ability to keep pace with another person. What happens when you and your beloved go on a walk together, engage in work together, or play a sport together? Can you keep up with each other? If not, the more active partner is likely to regard the other as a real party pooper. Lack of stamina often leads to limiting experiences that you and your beloved might share for mutual enjoyment.

ARE WE COMPATIBLE?

Laziness is not as much a matter of physical health as it is a matter of willpower. Is your beloved willing to do what it takes to get fit, stay fit, and be active?

Hygiene Is Basic to Compatibility

The person who bathes regularly generally can't stand to be intimate or live in close quarters with someone who doesn't. The same goes for washing hair, brushing teeth, and other matters of personal cleanliness and grooming.

Most young people put their best feet forward—and faces and hair and nails—when they first begin dating.

Be wary, however, if your beloved's concern about hygiene wanes the longer you date. The occasional grubby appearance is to be expected, but a trend of grubbiness is not. Ask yourself, Where does this trend lead?

Age as a Product of Fitness and Health

Although not directly something a person can control, age tends to be related to fitness and health.

We've all known couples that were years apart in chronological age, yet because both were fit and healthy physically and emotionally, they seemed very compatible. Jane and Roger first met when Jane was a college senior and Roger was a widower at age thirty-eight.

Both recognized at the outset of their relationship that they needed to stay healthy and fit. They worked at it—together. Today, they are sixty-three and seventy-nine. They travel often, play tennis and golf on alternating days, and enjoy the occasional late-night swim. Both are in good health.

PHYSICAL COMPATIBILITY I

If you and your beloved have a significant age difference, take a close look at your health habits:

○ What are the biological (as opposed to chronological) ages? Have both of you taken good care of yourselves? Do you have good energy, good health, and mental alertness?

○ What can the younger one do that the older one cannot do? Does that matter to either of you?

○ How active are both of you? Is the older person dependent on the younger one for any degree of care?

An age difference is often more mental than physical. Sometimes people the same age can look and respond to life with very different outlooks, degrees of energy, or levels of health.

Envision life with your beloved ten years from now. Think ahead, then, to twenty years, thirty years, and beyond. What changes in your physical and sexual relationship are likely to occur with the passing years? These changes nearly always happen faster if an age difference is more than ten years. There are few exceptions. Seriously appraise whether you like the life you envision on the distant horizon.

Chapter 4

Physical Compatibility II: A Daily Ordering of Space and Time

Kelley came to me with a downcast heart one day and said with a sigh, "I just hadn't counted on our being roommates."

She and Cal had married just the month before. To her utter dismay, Cal left food, or the remains of it, wherever he took his last bite. He discarded clothes, socks, and shoes wherever he took them off. And he didn't know the meaning of capping the toothpaste, cleaning out a sink, picking up a towel, or closing a dresser drawer tightly.

Kelley was a neatnik. Cal, a slob. They were not naturally compatible in the least when it came to their sense of orderliness.

ARE WE COMPATIBLE?

"How could I have known?" Kelley asked, even though she knew that her question was too late. She was equally committed to finding a level of agreement with Cal to bridge their difference.

She had a point. Kelley and Cal were residential students living in the dormitories of their college. The only time Kelley had seen Cal's room was during once-a-semester open-house nights. Cal and his roommate had made an obvious effort to have their room presentable on those occasions.

"What is Cal's car like?" I asked. Kelley grimaced. "He trashes it, then cleans it up," she replied. Car maintenance is generally a good clue to the sense of order that a person requires. Rarely does a person have an extremely tidy automobile interior and a slovenly home interior. The exception may be if the car is less than six months old.

"And, too," I added, "you might have asked Cal's mother what his room was like at home."

"I did," Kelley said, "just last week. She apparently picked up after Cal all the time."

If your beloved one has an apartment or home, what state is it in when you stop by unexpectedly? What housekeeping skills does your future spouse have? Are you resentful of the time and effort that your beloved spends cleaning up, washing up, and sprucing up?

Clean or Tidy?

There's a difference between being clean and being tidy. Cleanliness refers to germs, dirt, and debris; it includes both the presence of undesirable items and the odor associated with them. Tidiness refers to order and whether things are kept neat and in place.

Some people have a tremendous tolerance for disarray as long as the environment is clean. Others need their surroundings to be both tidy and clean. Still others don't care about cleanliness very much as long as things "look good." How about you and your intended spouse? Do you have the same needs for cleanliness and order to feel comfortable in your dwelling place?

A Matter of Style

A home that is truly a haven must be comfortable. And to be comfortable, it must have colors, textures, and styles pleasing to the occupants.

A part of comfort involves what I call *clutter tolerance.* Some people require vast expanses of smooth surface, whether floor, table top, shelf, or wall. Others like to have almost every square foot of space filled with pictures, plants, wall hangings, books, vases, and memorabilia or artifacts. To one eye, the abundance of items in a room is going to look like clutter. To another, a creative eclectic mix that makes for a lived-in feel.

Some people need lots of light in their environment. Others like a dark, library feel.

Take a look at the way your beloved presently has his or her home decorated, even if that home is only a dorm room or a garage apartment. Go shopping together. Visit model homes. Look for trends in each other. Can you find a way to accommodate what both like?

Note especially if one seems more reluctant than the other to compromise. How tenaciously does either one hold opinions? Reaching agreement is nearly always possible in matters of style, texture, and color if each person is willing to work on agreement.

Who Decides?

In forging a common life, spouses face a host of questions about how to order shared living space. Only some issues are decorative. Other issues relate to accessibility. The core issue, however, is one of control. Who gets to decide what goes where and how the place appears?

Compatibility is affected when both people feel a vested interest in these decisions. When both care, conflicts are almost inevitable.

How can you tell in advance if you will be able to resolve differences about organization and decoration prior to marriage? First, determine who cares most about what. Many people care only about certain aspects of organization and decoration, and not others. If both care about overlapping areas, are you willing to relinquish at least some of the decision-making power to your beloved? Do you demand input?

Also ask, What general patterns of organization does my beloved have in his or her current abode? Are things clustered together but not kept in pristine order? Is everything in its place and only in its place? Is there a general sense of disorganization? Is my beloved willing to change or to give up some current possessions? Am I?

In blending two lives together, you will nearly always find duplicates, whether in the record collection or an endowment of kitchen appliances. Which set will you keep? What will you give away, throw away, or donate? Agreement is possible in this area, even if you don't automatically experience harmony!

Different Schedules Can Affect Compatibility

Of equal importance to the ordering of space is the ordering of time. Do you and your beloved have similar schedules? If not, what can you do to accommodate the differences?

Tina is vitally concerned about punctuality. Frank has probably never been on time in his life, apart from Tina's prodding. Tina, on the other hand, can't stand to be late. She classified Frank's attitude as one that reflected great disrespect for others. "He doesn't value their time, so he must not value them," she said to me.

Tina and Frank never did find agreement. She is now married to Lee, who managed to show up on time for every one of their dates. Frank is married to Cindy, who is also a late arriver. She is delighted that Frank never pesters her to hurry up.

People move through life at different paces, according to different biological clocks, and with different expectations about timing.

Ask yourself, Do I have to wait a lot for my beloved? How do I feel about that? Do I constantly feel hurried or pressured to speed up my life? Do both of us seem to be most active, alert, and vibrant during the same hours of the day? What kind of schedule does my future spouse presently keep? Is it a schedule that I would find comfortable?

Being out of phase with each other can be extremely disorienting, and can affect everything from eating and sleeping schedules to friendships, mutual activities, and times of heightened sexuality. Timing differences aren't insurmountable, but they are difficult adjustments to make. Are both of you willing to make the effort required?

Compatibility in the Management of Material Goods and Property

Marriage counselors have noted for several decades that most of the problems they encounter are related to one of two things: sex or money. The management of money includes earning power, spending habits, spending priorities, honesty in business transactions, and the maintenance of property. Each affects compatibility.

Earning *Is* Power to Some

Nearly all young married couples work and work hard. And rarely do the two partners in a marriage earn the same amount. This discrepancy can result in competition, resentment, frustration, or manipulative behavior—any of which can greatly affect compatibility.

You and your intended spouse need to talk candidly about what you earn and about the financial and physical assets that you bring to your marriage. How will you manage the total sum of what you have and what you earn? Will it all go into one pot with equal access by both? Will you have separate accounts, each responsible for a portion of the bills? Will you have three accounts: his, hers, and ours?

In most cases, the issue is not how much each person earns, but whether each person is contributing in an equi-

PHYSICAL COMPATIBILITY II

table fashion to the mutual benefit of both and whether each person has discretionary money to spend.

By contributing equitably, I don't necessarily mean contributing equally. Of great concern to most people in planning the family budget is the amount of discretionary money available for private use. Each partner needs a certain amount of money to spend without accounting to the other partner.

Allow a little "fun money," pocket money, whimsy change, or whatever you call it for each person as you divide your earnings.

Even more basic than who earns what is the issue of whether both parties are working, at what, and how many hours a week.

Rene's fiancé, Roy, was a workaholic. He put in about seventy hours a week in his graphic arts business. He brought home a six-figure annual income as his reward. Rene appreciated Roy's talent, business savvy, and earning power, but she resented the fact that she hardly ever saw him. Roy came to the conclusion that Rene was more important to him than his nonstop work schedule.

Roy hired two assistants, which cut his income just about in half. He reduced his work hours to fifty a week, and went in pursuit of Rene. She was thrilled at the chance to resume their relationship on a different footing. They married a few months later, and over time, Rene also began working in his business as a secretary and bookkeeper. She sees Roy now more than she ever has, and she doesn't mind the ten- and twelve-hour days that they sometimes put in at the shop.

Virginia, a surgeon, married her hairdresser, Cliff. Apart from their chosen careers, they had a great amount of compatibility going into their relationship. Both were successful, worked hard, and enjoyed what they did for a living. Virginia, however, earned about three times what Cliff earned in a year. Cliff was uncomfortable with that discrepancy, and so was Virginia until they came to an agreement. They decided to live on Cliff's income and use all of Virginia's income for retirement-oriented investments and luxuries.

You and your intended spouse need to carefully evaluate the value you place on work, the amount of time you intend to devote to work (and what impact that might have on your family life), the amount that you earn, and whether you are working in jobs that you enjoy and that bring a sense of accomplishment.

Ask yourselves, Do we have the same work ethic? Are we working at jobs we enjoy and value? Are we able to find a way of equitably sharing the mutual expenses we will have as a couple?

Of greatest importance, of course, is the degree to which both value work and are intent on developing careers.

Spending Habits Encompass Budgeting and Quality Factors

Some people manage money well. Others don't. Therein lie most of the money conflicts in a marriage.

The excellent money manager purchases only what she can afford, with a minimal use of credit and a maximum effort to save until she has enough to pay cash for an item. The lousy money manager overextends and is perpetually in debt.

Physical Compatibility II

Kenny was meticulous in keeping a budget and living within it. But if Ursula had a penny in her pocket, she found a way to spend it. They faced their incompatibility in this area early on in their dating relationship. Kenny saw no hope for a marriage with Ursula, even though he was crazy about her. Saving and investing were very important to him. Ursula, on the other hand, saw Kenny as being too tight-fisted with money.

The day came, however, when a sum of money that Ursula had counted on receiving didn't arrive, but her bills did. She struggled greatly with not being able to pay her bills on time. She agreed to give living-within-a-budget a try. It was confining and painful at first, but then she began to enjoy a feeling of greater control over her finances. She still isn't much into investing, but she is out of debt and has opened a savings account.

Kenny and Ursula have set a wedding date, and part of their financial agreement is that Kenny will keep the books and hold the credit cards. Ursula will have her own checking account and will deposit half of what she earns into their shared account. She will be able to spend the other half in whatever way she wants by means of her own checking account. Both seem happy with this agreement.

Apart from how much one spends is the matter of "for what" one spends. People have vastly different outlooks on quality and the importance of purchasing the best versus purchasing the most.

Clarise purchased only the best. She shopped in the best stores and bought very little, but what she bought was always in exquisite taste and of the finest quality. She fell in

ARE WE COMPATIBLE?

love with Gary, who was Mr. Bargain Basement. Gary purchased everything in a warehouse, at a garage sale, or at a 75 percent off sale. Both spent about the same amount of money on stuff. Gary had hoards of material possessions, Clarise very little. Both were happy with their things and had little respect for the items purchased by the other.

Their agreement prior to their marriage included separate checking accounts and a split of responsibilities for purchasing various items. Five years into their marriage, they had developed a mutual appreciation for what each had accomplished.

Take a look at your beloved's current purchasing habits, and ask, Is he or she into only designer labels and famous brands? Does my beloved drive twenty miles to save twenty cents? Does my beloved know how to make a budget and live accordingly? Is his or her bank account regularly overdrawn? Are the credit cards maxed out? How important is quality to each of us? How important is a bargain?

Where Will the Money Go?

Directly related to spending habits are spending priorities. On what will you spend your earnings?

Ask, What will we save? What will we invest? Will we be generous in making contributions to the church or community funds? To what percentage? What percentage of our earnings do we anticipate devoting to our home?

Some young couples immediately want to invest in a house. Others are content to live in an apartment and acquire furniture and appliances, even as they save for a house. Still others opt for a condominium lease and weekend excursions rather than a home and weekend yard work.

PHYSICAL COMPATIBILITY II

Ask, How much will go for monthly payments? How much will we allot for food and clothes? How much will be set aside for entertainment, recreation, and travel? These decisions vary widely from couple to couple. The important issue to compatibility is, Who controls the spending priorities?

Hannah and Patrick were as harmonious a couple in this area as I have ever encountered. They had no trouble pooling their incomes—which were only about three thousand dollars apart in annual salary—and following the same guide as a married couple. Their breakdown was 10 percent given in contributions, 10 percent to savings, 30 percent on housing, 30 percent on utilities and consumables (including food), 10 percent on car payments and maintenance, and 10 percent for entertainment, trips, and leisure pursuits.

Carmen and Paulo had no priorities related to money when they married. They paid bills as they came due, and if they had money left over at the month's end, they splurged. The day came, however, when Carmen became pregnant. The couple faced for the first time in their lives the prospect of making a budget. They consulted a financial adviser, and with her help, they devised a plan.

Prioritizing their spending opened their eyes to new ways in which they were compatible, and in the end, it strengthened their marriage during a crisis that might otherwise have put stress on their relationship.

Ask yourselves as you prepare for marriage, Do we have the same general priorities on how money is to be managed? Are we able to agree about who will set the priorities for our spending?

ARE WE COMPATIBLE?

Honest Business Transactions

To conduct personal business honestly, one must keep records and file taxes. If one partner in a marriage is a meticulous record keeper, and the other partner has never saved a receipt, they will face a very practical problem almost immediately.

Decide early in your planning for marriage who is going to keep the books. Will both write checks out of the same account? How will you keep track of the balance? Will both make decisions regarding investments, such as stocks, certificates of deposit, or mutual funds? Will both use the same credit cards? If so, you need a system to keep your records straight.

Ask yourselves, Who will be doing our taxes? What receipts do we need to keep? How will we justify our records should we be audited by the IRS? Should I die before my spouse, will our financial records be clear and easily audited? These are all questions that you need to answer up front and candidly.

At the time Ruth's husband died, she was in for a rude awakening regarding their finances. Through the fifteen years of their marriage, Ruth balanced their checkbook. Her husband, Dan, managed the credit cards. Ruth noticed periodic deposits made into the checking account for rather substantial amounts, but she assumed that the deposits were related to his job as a pharmaceutical salesman. Ruth had no idea that Dan had been drawing cash advances on credit cards to make the deposits, and that she and her husband were in credit-card debt to the tune of nearly thirty thousand dollars at the time of his death!

Physical Compatibility II

It took Ruth five years to dig herself out from under the mound of indebtedness. With her financial freedom came a strong resolve, "If I marry again, *I'm* managing all of the finances, or else I'll insist on a monthly accounting."

Honesty is vital to trust. And without trust, there's little hope for a relationship to endure.

Maintaining What You Acquire

Once items are purchased and investments made, the hard work of maintenance begins. For most things in life—including a marriage—much less is required for acquisition than for maintenance.

Does your beloved take care of belongings? Are the possessions in his or her life in good working order? Does your beloved seek to purchase a replacement item the minute something goes wrong with an object? Is he or she quick to throw things away? Does your beloved maintain things regularly?

The way a person maintains possessions is often similar to the way a person maintains a relationship.

Zena discovered quickly in her relationship with Cameron that they were on two different wavelengths. She was forever retrieving things that he was preparing to discard. "The item might have been nicked a little or had a little rip in a seam," she told me. "I knew we had a big difference when his car came through a major wind storm with a golf-ball-sized ding in the roof. He was ready to trade it in for a new car!"

"And you broke up with him over that?" I asked.

"It said a lot to me," she said. "If he was going to demand that much perfection in things, he probably was going to demand that much perfection in me. The day he saw me as

ARE WE COMPATIBLE?

being flawed was probably going to be the last day of our relationship anyway."

A couple intent on marriage should discuss who will do most of the maintenance. Is one person expecting the other to do all of the laundry, mending, dusting, mopping, vacuuming, polishing, and so forth? How will the maintenance chores be divided? Can each allow the other full freedom to maintain certain items or do certain chores and be satisfied with the efforts?

One young couple divides the maintenance chores this way: he takes care of everything related to the floors and walls, and she takes care of the rest. Another couple alternates cooking and cleaning-up chores. Yet another couple lists all the chores that need to be done each week, and each takes a turn picking which ones to do on a one-for-you, one-for-me basis.

There are lots of ways to find agreement in this area, but the main issues are these: Do both place the same value on the care of possessions, and at what point do you seek to replace them?

And Now for a Physical Compatibility Quiz!

In each compatibility area, we will close with a brief quiz—not a quiz with right or wrong answers or one that yields a good or bad grade. Rather, the quiz is a method of appraising your relationship, a means for both to take stock of attitudes and values, and to compare them in a way that is visual and that readily shows areas of natural compatibility and incompatibility.

PHYSICAL COMPATIBILITY II

Identical forms are provided for the "Physical Compatibility Quiz." One is for you to complete, in privacy; the other is for your beloved to complete.

On most forms, here and elsewhere in the book, you will be asked to make an X to indicate your position on each of a number of continuums between two statements, generally opposites. An example of a continuum is given below:

The person who marked this continuum obviously likes sweet tastes more than sour ones.

As you mark your responses, do so quickly. Go with your first instinct. Also, mark the response more toward the extreme than you think you might otherwise. People tend to gravitate toward a middle position when marking forms. Push your opinions toward the edges.

If you say, "Well, I like both, under different circumstances," back away and try to take your life as a whole. If you could have only *one* position for all circumstances, which would be most comfortable to you?

Mark your forms now.

PHYSICAL COMPATIBILITY QUIZ

PERSON A

Mark your position with an X on each continuum. Exaggerate your position slightly in favor of the choice you make. Recognize that both are "I like" positions.

I like . . .

physical closeness		physical space
fantasy		reality
innocence		experience
being touched by others		being touched only if I initiate it
predictability		surprises
lots of talk		lots of silence
having my way		following a strong leader
planning all things		not planning
details		global views
to talk about sex		*not* to talk about sex
uniformity		variety
cleaning up		making a mess
being strong and in control		being vulnerable and available
even spacing		uneven spacing
openness		closeness
mornings		nights
being on a schedule		going with the flow
seeing what happens		being able to predict
fixing the old		buying all new
balconies		caves

PHYSICAL COMPATIBILITY QUIZ
PERSON B

Mark your position with an X on each continuum. Exaggerate your position slightly in favor of the choice you make. Recognize that both are "I like" positions.

I like . . .

physical closeness	|———|———|———|———|———|———|———|———|———|	physical space
fantasy	|———|———|———|———|———|———|———|———|———|	reality
innocence	|———|———|———|———|———|———|———|———|———|	experience
being touched by others	|———|———|———|———|———|———|———|———|———|	being touched only if I initiate it
predictability	|———|———|———|———|———|———|———|———|———|	surprises
lots of talk	|———|———|———|———|———|———|———|———|———|	lots of silence
having my way	|———|———|———|———|———|———|———|———|———|	following a strong leader
planning all things	|———|———|———|———|———|———|———|———|———|	not planning
details	|———|———|———|———|———|———|———|———|———|	global views
to talk about sex	|———|———|———|———|———|———|———|———|———|	*not* to talk about sex
uniformity	|———|———|———|———|———|———|———|———|———|	variety
cleaning up	|———|———|———|———|———|———|———|———|———|	making a mess
being strong and in control	|———|———|———|———|———|———|———|———|———|	being vulnerable and available
even spacing	|———|———|———|———|———|———|———|———|———|	uneven spacing
openness	|———|———|———|———|———|———|———|———|———|	closeness
mornings	|———|———|———|———|———|———|———|———|———|	nights
being on a schedule	|———|———|———|———|———|———|———|———|———|	going with the flow
seeing what happens	|———|———|———|———|———|———|———|———|———|	being able to predict
fixing the old	|———|———|———|———|———|———|———|———|———|	buying all new
balconies	|———|———|———|———|———|———|———|———|———|	caves

ARE WE COMPATIBLE?

Evaluating Your Responses

Transfer the responses from both forms to the third form, "Your Physical Compatibility as a Couple." Don't worry about keeping track as to which response belongs to which person.

Then connect the positions in a vertical fashion as shown on the samples below:

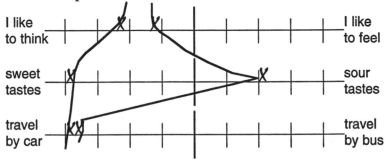

After you have connected the marks, go back to chapter 2 and take another look at "Compatibility Model A." Can you see how the gaps in your responses on this form are similar to the gaps between the two people in the general model?

Even though some of the responses may have been to the left side of the continuums, and others to the right, the gap between your two opinions is the important area. Are you and your beloved wide apart on virtually all of the continuums? Are the responses to these aspects of life similar? Where are the most significant differences?

Most important, begin to talk about what you might be able to do to bridge your areas of difference with an agreement. (You may want to jump ahead and read chapter 9.)

Rejoice in the areas where you have natural harmony!

YOUR PHYSICAL COMPATIBILITY
AS A COUPLE

Transfer both sets of responses to this form. It does not matter which marks belong to which person.

We like . . .

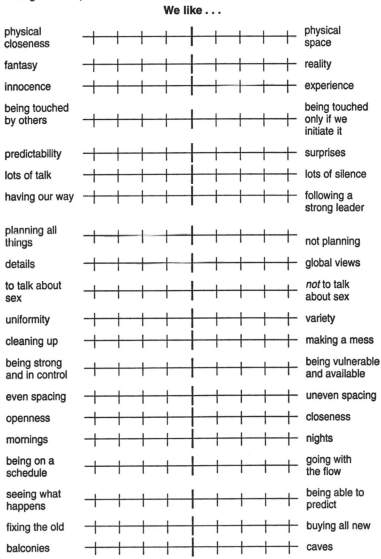

physical closeness	physical space
fantasy	reality
innocence	experience
being touched by others	being touched only if we initiate it
predictability	surprises
lots of talk	lots of silence
having our way	following a strong leader
planning all things	not planning
details	global views
to talk about sex	*not* to talk about sex
uniformity	variety
cleaning up	making a mess
being strong and in control	being vulnerable and available
even spacing	uneven spacing
openness	closeness
mornings	nights
being on a schedule	going with the flow
seeing what happens	being able to predict
fixing the old	buying all new
balconies	caves

ARE WE COMPATIBLE?

Physical compatibility is only one of five broad areas of compatibility covered in this book. Don't be devastated if you find points of incompatibility. Although physical compatibility is a multifaceted area, it is an area in which agreement is probably the easiest to reach.

This is not to say that physical incompatibility should be dismissed or underestimated in importance. As a married couple, you and your beloved will be living together physically (at least in the vast majority of instances). Although the problems of physical incompatibility may not be the most cosmic, they tend to be the most numerous and frequently occurring problems.

Find a way of reaching agreement about physical incompatibility, and you and your beloved are likely to find a way of surmounting most other problems.

Chapter 5

COMPATIBILITY OF BACKGROUND

When we are dealing with background, we are dealing with what was and its impact on what is. When we are talking about uniting two lives, we are also attempting to project what will be. The past does not necessarily predict the future. At the same time, we must never discount the past.

We also need to consider that we do not create a background all by ourselves. Others are involved—family, friends, neighbors, associates. We are, to a great extent, what others have influenced us or genetically endowed us to be. We cannot change certain things about our lives. We can change other things but, in many cases, shouldn't.

Be cautious if your beloved says to you, "I can change," or "It won't be that way in the future," especially if you are dealing with a lifelong pattern or circumstance.

Be especially wary, too, if your beloved seeks to cut off

parents, family, or longtime friends for your sake. Your beloved is always going to be connected to those people to some degree. Their elimination would likely leave your beloved feeling diminished in identity.

The five main areas to consider with regard to background are these: (1) race and tribe, (2) cultural heritage (including religion), (3) socioeconomic factors, (4) education, and (5) life experiences. We'll take each in turn.

Area Number 1: Race and Tribe

Race and tribe are coupled here because conflicts within a race of people can be just as vitriolic and entrenched as those existing between races.

Many people assume that races and tribes should remain pure; there should be no interracial or intertribal marriages. Most racial and tribal prejudice is deep-seated and, to a great extent, historical. Prejudice tends to be handed down from generation to generation, with the bitterness increasing over time.

Also a historical fact, however, is that interracial and intertribal marriages have existed for millennia and, in some cases, were highly desired. Moses married a non-Hebrew woman, and so did Boaz in marrying Ruth.

In many parts of the world, and especially in the United States, a significant percentage of the population is of mixed race, and probably the vast majority is mixed in tribe—for example, those who have German and English ancestry, or Dutch and Danish ancestry.

Attitudes about interracial and intertribal marriages vary

COMPATIBILITY OF BACKGROUND

widely from region to region in the United States, and in other nations. In the Caribbean nations, for example, interracial marriages are quite common. In Japan, they are virtually taboo. Within our own nation and even city and state, it is not uncommon to find a family with high racial prejudice living next door to a family of low racial prejudice.

Very few of us marry a person who has exactly our same racial or tribal background. Primary concerns should be

- the attitude of each person about his or her race and tribe.
- the attitude of each person about his or her potential spouse's race and tribe.
- the attitude of each person about the mixing of the two bloodlines.

Beyond the opinions of those who are to be married are the concerns of family members and, to a significant extent, the opinions of close friends. Ask, therefore, How do I value my race? How do I value the race of my intended spouse? How do I value the mixing of our races? (The answer to this question will determine, in part, your attitude toward any children you might bear.) How do my family members and friends regard the mixing of our bloodlines?

The feelings of family members and friends might be bridged in a number of ways: information, association over time, prayer, travel (to experience other cultures), exposure to varied cultural ceremonies (including those of the future in-law's culture), and so forth.

Be wary of the person who says, "I love you in spite of

ARE WE COMPATIBLE?

your race," or "I love you because of your race." If race is not an issue, it won't be brought up. Also be wary if you sense that your beloved is critical of your race or tribe as a whole and holds you as an exception.

Area Number 2: Cultural Heritage

Our culture includes our language, social structures, customs and traditions, and religion.

Language

Eva was engaged to Jirka when I first met her. She was from Norway, he from what was then Czechoslovakia. They met while both were college students in the United States. Both were beginners in English, their only common language. Listening to their conversations was an amazing experience. They communicated, but much of what they said to each other obviously was nonverbal!

They eventually married, and with the Russian invasion of Prague in the late 1960s, they chose to stay in the United States, with periodic visits to Norway. Over time, both became fluent in English. Eva said to me not too long ago, "I sometimes wonder what we said to each other in those first couple of years. I finally decided that it wasn't enough that we both knew English. I needed to learn some Czech, and Jirka needed to learn some Norwegian."

Most linguists will tell you that it is virtually impossible to separate language from the way people think, including the way they process information and form opinions. The greater the difference in language structure, the greater the differ-

COMPATIBILITY OF BACKGROUND

ence in thought patterns. Keep that in mind if you are marrying a person whose native language is different from your own.

Family Structures

Culture includes family structures. Ask about your intended spouse, Is my beloved's family close-knit? What is the structure of the family? Who is dominant? What roles does each family member have?

Some cultures place great importance on the role of grandparents; others don't. Some cultures tend to have large families, with frequent contact among family members. Other cultures have smaller, more isolated family units. Some cultures are heavily dominated by Papa, others by Mama.

Don't discount cultural influences in the way families are structured. Your beloved probably anticipates structuring your family just as his or her own was structured, with the same unspoken rules in effect. If you and your beloved are from divergent cultures, you are likely in for a struggle.

Customs and Traditions

Customs and traditions invariably require agreement if the partners in a marriage are from differing cultures. Some customs are national. If you grew up in the United States and you marry a person from a different country, he or she won't understand much about Thanksgiving Day, the Fourth of July, Labor Day, or Memorial Day.

Some customs are rooted in particular families. My family had a custom of visiting a certain amusement park the first day of summer vacation. Our next-door neighbors had a cus-

ARE WE COMPATIBLE?

tom of going camping each summer. We counted on these summertime customs to remain a part of our lives!

Other customs are rooted in religion. Lauren met her husband, Ib (short for Ibrahim), while both were employed by an oil company in Houston. In the corporate culture there, they saw little difference between themselves, even though Lauren had grown up in Texas and Ib in Lebanon. Neither was very religious.

Three years into the marriage, Ib was introduced to two new workers from Lebanon, and the three formed an almost immediate bond of friendship. Ib's two new friends were deeply religious and kept all of the Islamic customs and holidays. Before long, Ib was asking Lauren to wear long sleeves, cover her head in public, attend mosque services with him, and study the Koran. She obliged, all the while maintaining a certain degree of emotional distance.

The day came when Ib insisted that Lauren convert fully to Islam as a prior condition to their having children. He began to speak more frequently of returning to Lebanon in the near future, perhaps to stay. Lauren could not comply. Converting to Islam meant giving up too much of her own culture. They parted ways, but not without a great deal of emotional pain.

All religions have customs and traditions that affect culture. In Lauren's case, one thing she missed most during the last two years of her marriage to Ib was the celebration of Christmas with her family.

Not all religious differences are as profound as those experienced by Ib and Lauren. Conflicts can arise from denominational differences within a particular religion. For example, in a marriage between a Baptist and a Methodist, a conflict might arise about method of baptism.

When it comes to traditions, customs, and religion, the key questions to ask yourselves are these: How can both of us maintain our faith and still have a commonality of custom and tradition in our home? If we have children, in which religion will they be reared? Which holidays or festivals are we going to celebrate and in what manner? What cultural differences do we have, and how will we blend those differences to create, in effect, a third culture in our home? Or will one culture dominate to the exclusion of the other? How do we intend to include our parents and friends in our practice of religion?

These are tough questions, and they often need to be answered during formal premarital counseling with a member of the clergy of one or both of the religions represented by you and your beloved. Allow enough time in premarital counseling for all of your questions to be answered fully.

Area Number 3: Socioeconomic Factors

A number of cultural anthropologists contend that socioeconomic factors separate people far more than cultural or racial and tribal factors. They point to the fact that rich people in Culture A often relate more readily to rich people in Culture B than they do to poor people in their own culture. Poor people in Culture A have more in common with poor people around the world than with middle-class or rich people in their own culture, and the same principle holds for the middle-class people of the world.

Rich people around the world tend to have the greatest

ARE WE COMPATIBLE?

power within their communities (unless members of another social class vastly outnumber them and are mobilized by strong leadership). They tend to have the most material possessions and the greatest access to professional and practical services. They tend to enjoy the best health.

Poor people, by contrast, tend to have the weakest political voice, the fewest goods, the least access to genuine help, and the poorest health.

We've all heard the sad love songs about the impossible love between a rich girl and a poor boy, but often, the socioeconomic difference does not need to be millions of dollars versus pennies for a conflict to arise. The difference can be much less profound.

Sarah grew up in what she considered a middle-class home in a small town in California. While attending an out-of-state college, she met Tommy, who had grown up in what he considered a middle-class home in a small town in Arkansas. Sarah and Tommy had the same major in college, were both bright and hardworking, and shared many of the same goals and dreams for their lives. Sarah was continually amazed, however, at what Tommy did *not* know about or know how to do. Tommy wasn't up on the latest fads, he didn't know how to work the newest gadgets, he occasionally used poor grammar, and he simply wasn't "hip"—from Sarah's perspective. Sarah began to see Tommy as being beneath her on the social ladder.

When one person sees another as being "less than" or "not as good as," a dangerous weed begins to grow in a relationship. Just as in the areas of race, tribe, culture, and religion, what matters regarding socioeconomic differences are not the differences themselves but our perceptions of the differences and our strong opinions about people we view as being different or inferior.

Sarah broke off her relationship with Tommy. She didn't think that he would ever be able to "overcome his roots," in her terms. Tommy was brokenhearted, but with the passage of time, he began to see that he could not have tolerated Sarah's condescending attitude. As far as he was concerned, he was a fine person with high morals, a solid background, and a lot of potential—and fortunately for him, that's exactly the way Bonnie saw him, too. Sarah married "up" the social ladder, a young man from a wealthy family.

Ask yourself about your beloved, Does my beloved ever put me down about my social manners or chide me for inappropriate behavior? Am I truly "at home" in his or her world? What material possessions and practical or professional services did my beloved have as a child or teen that I did not have? Do I ever think about my beloved as being inferior? Are there times when I am embarrassed by something my beloved does or says? If we had to move next door to one set of parents, which set would we choose? In other words, which neighborhood would we want to live in? Why?

Area Number 4: Education

The exact degree each person has earned is not nearly as important as the degree to which both value education and continue to learn new things. Some high-school graduates are extremely well read and have a substantial amount of self-education. Some college grads haven't cracked a book since graduation day.

ARE WE COMPATIBLE?

Information comes in a variety of ways: magazines, television programs, newspapers, books, academic journals, conversations with informed sources, trial-and-error research. And the desire to acquire information and to grow intellectually need not diminish with age.

Travel is an educational experience. Travel broadens horizons and forces an individual to face many personal prejudices, the ability to be flexible and adaptable, and the frustrations regarding time and space. If you have traveled a great deal, and your beloved hasn't been out of his or her hometown, your world is much larger than that of your beloved. You have abundant skills and insights that your beloved doesn't have.

Ask as you prepare to marry, Do both of us value education in the same way? Is each willing to allow the other enough intellectual space? Can each of us appreciate the other's different learning style or the way to process information? Are we alive intellectually, continuing to explore life and study new bodies of information?

Be wary if one of you places very high value on education and continued learning, and the other doesn't.

Area Number 5: Life Experiences

Vastly different life experiences can lead to incompatibility in numerous ways. Very often an age difference is problematic not so much for the years that have gone by but for what has gone into the years.

These previous life experiences can be especially troublesome to a couple:

COMPATIBILITY OF BACKGROUND

o Past abuse of chemical substances

o A prior marriage or children from previous relationships

o A criminal record

o Involvement in a cult

o Bankruptcy

o Hospitalization for psychological problems

o Major illness or accident

o Abuse (physical, sexual, or emotional, including rape or being the victim of a crime)

You need to know if your beloved has had any of these life experiences. Even though the experience may have been long ago in the past, your beloved probably still bears certain emotional scars that will affect the relationship.

Of these experiences, a prior marriage and the birth of children in a previous relationship may never fully be in the past. A prior spouse and present children can represent very real responsibilities that can diminish substantially the financial, emotional, and time resources that you desire to have all to yourself.

You need to get answers to these questions: What led your beloved to this experience? What has your beloved actively done to recover from the experience? And does your beloved own up to his or her part in the mistake or failure?

Underlying Causes

Something caused your beloved one to drink too much, take drugs, get involved in criminal activity, get overextended to the point of bankruptcy, or be drawn to a cult. There were reasons your beloved married who and when he or she did. There was probably a buildup of some kind prior to hospitalization for emotional disorders or the diagnosis of a major illness.

As you listen to your beloved's explanation of the reasons, evaluate on the basis of your relationship whether the tendencies still exist. Does your beloved still struggle with loneliness, peer pressure, lust, greed, or any of a host of underlying motivations that may have led to the error?

Active Recovery

Your beloved should have sought help after the hurt or tragedy. How was he able to readjust his thinking after involvement in a cult? What type of program helped her with her addiction or chemical-abuse problem? How did she overcome bitterness and anger in the wake of a divorce? What steps has your beloved taken to right his finances; what changes has he made in the way he manages money?

The old adage that time heals simply isn't true. Time may cause a memory to fade, but it doesn't heal. Some people who experienced tragedies or mistakes decades ago are more bitter about them today than ever before.

Be very concerned if there has been no active therapy program. Without an active recovery process, the problem has gone underground. The stuffed emotions and repressed memories will erupt someday, and you may well be a witness to them.

Justification of Past Behavior

How does your beloved justify this negative experience in her life? How has she resolved the difficulty emotionally and spiritually?

Does he blame others for what happened to him? Is he still

living with feelings of unforgiveness, bitterness, or revenge? Does he still show anger or hatred?

Does she accept partial blame in problems that involved relationships into which she voluntarily entered? Be wary if your beloved accepts none of the blame or attempts to shoulder all of the blame. Neither is a realistic position regarding a marriage, a business partnership, involvement in a cult, gang activity, or situations that involved others.

Does your beloved hold a realistic viewpoint toward what happened? Is the event fully in the past? Does it continue to haunt him or her, perhaps in the form of nightmares, painful memories, outbursts of anger or terror, or various dysfunctional behaviors? If so, the healing process is not complete, and you need to know that you will be entering that healing process with your beloved should you marry.

Be wary if your beloved's response to the past event is anything other than repentance, sorrow, forgiveness extended to all other persons who may have been involved, and a receiving of divine forgiveness.

Relationships with Family and Friends

Earlier in this chapter I alluded to the compatibility of cultural heritage and the way in which families might be structured. Family and friends affect compatibility in other ways, too. The focus in this section is on how family members and friends have related and presently relate to your beloved.

Life experiences, education, and cultural traditions do not happen apart from family and friends. Your beloved has not existed in a vacuum, waiting for your arrival in his or her life.

ARE WE COMPATIBLE?

Your beloved has already formed attachments, some of them quite strong, to other people.

Family

In looking at your beloved's immediate family, note these five relationships:

1. *Your beloved's relationship with the parent of the same sex (that is, male with Father, female with Mother).* If your beloved has a good relationship with this parent—marked by good communication, mutual admiration, and warm memories—there is a great likelihood that your beloved is going to be like this parent as the years pass. If your beloved does not have a good relationship with this parent, he or she is going to rebel against the parent's example. Be concerned if there is no role model that your beloved is seeking to emulate.

2. *Your beloved's relationship with the parent of the opposite sex (that is, male with Mother, female with Father).* This relationship is likely to reflect the way that your beloved is going to treat you. If a young man shows great respect and tenderness toward his mother, he probably will show the same to his bride. If he has contempt for his mother or ignores her, you can expect the same treatment if you become his wife. If a young woman trusts her father, extends care and compassion toward him, and admires him, you will likely receive the same treatment if you become her husband. If she deplores her father's behavior or resents his absence from her life, you may be the object of the same feelings.

Be wary if your beloved finds no fault in the parent of the opposite sex. That is the mark of an unrealistic and, therefore, unhealthy relationship.

COMPATIBILITY OF BACKGROUND

Your beloved's appreciation for the parent of the opposite sex can create a pitfall if your beloved expects you to be like that parent in all that you do. In a marriage, partners are in a position to help each other, not parent each other.

3. *Your beloved's relationship with older or same-age siblings.* Was he or she jealous of siblings? Highly competitive? Close in communication and contact? Respectful? Your friends and siblings are likely to be treated the same way.

4. **Your beloved's relationship with aunts and uncles.** Your parents will probably be treated in this way as in-laws. Although young people often call their spouses' parents by endearing "Mom and Dad" terms, the more realistic characterization of the relationship is that of a beloved aunt and uncle. Don't expect your future spouse to love your parents as you do—nor to hate them as you might. He has no long-standing relationship with them. She is more likely to regard them as a loving and benevolent aunt and uncle or as a meddlesome aunt and uncle whose opinions can be dismissed.

5. **Your beloved's relationship with younger siblings.** That is something of an indicator of the way your spouse is likely to treat your children. Did your beloved find younger siblings to be a pain in the neck, creatures to be avoided, or objects of intense jealousy? If so, your beloved may very well criticize the time you spend with your children or the affection you openly bestow on them, be impatient as a parent, or resent their presence. If your beloved enjoyed playing with younger siblings and felt responsibility for their welfare, he or she is likely to have that same intuitive response to your children.

These guidelines are not absolutes, of course. Be observant. And be objective.

ARE WE COMPATIBLE?

Friends

Also note how your beloved treats close friends. Does your beloved have friends? Many or few? Close or distant emotionally? Nearby or faraway? Does your beloved have long-standing friends? Are there people with whom he or she has had a relationship over a significant number of years?

Your beloved's long-standing friendships can be revealing about your beloved's capacity for loyalty and ability to "ride out" a relationship through both difficult and joyous times.

Close friends aren't going to disappear once you are married. If there are close friends you can't stand, you are going to have to find some way of accommodating them in your life.

Does your beloved insist on having exclusive friendships—ones in which you are not invited to participate? If so, be concerned. Your beloved is limiting your access to his or her life.

How influential are your beloved's friends when it comes to your beloved's choices, opinions, and behaviors? If you believe that your beloved is controlled by a particular friend, be wary. No matter what you say, you are not likely to break that control or diminish the person's hold on your beloved. Your criticism of such a friend is likely to be seen as too harsh or unfounded.

The Roommate Track Record

Take a look at your beloved's track record with roommates.

How does your beloved speak of past roommates? The

person who speaks well of past roommates is likely to genuinely enjoy getting to know others and has the capacity to see good qualities in all people. These are admirable traits that enhance the probability that the two of you will be able to bridge your compatibility gaps and forge agreements.

In general, the person who has fairly few, close, and long-standing friendships and roommates is much more ready for a committed marriage relationship than the person who has many, shallow, and recent friendships or abundant short stints with roommates.

The Value Placed on the Past

As your beloved one speaks about the past, note the tone of voice. Does he speak lovingly of friends and family members? Does he genuinely like and appreciate who he is, how he was raised, and the people who have been influential in his life?

Ask, Does my beloved regard the past as a good foundation or a shaky one? Does my beloved dismiss the past or seek to forget it? Does he dwell on the past and desire to return to it? (Both are unhealthy positions if taken to the extreme.) Does my beloved wish she could change who she is? Why? In what ways?

Your intended spouse's regard for the past is just as important as the past itself. The opinions and feelings about the past will affect most directly the relationship that you share.

Be very concerned if your future spouse contends that the past doesn't matter. It does. It is the foundation on which both of your lives have been built, and ultimately, it is the

ARE WE COMPATIBLE?

foundation on which your future life rests as a married couple. It is the heritage that your children will be given.

The Time Has Come for a Background Compatibility Quiz

The "Background Compatibility Quiz" is somewhat different from the quiz you took in the chapter on physical compatibility.

The continuums are labeled as the example below:

Perfect agreement would be noted by the X placed above. Both partners in the upcoming marriage might have had dogs as pets, for example.

On the continuum below, the person marking the form indicates that he and his intended spouse did not share the same childhood pets and that the pets were vastly different. This mark indicates not only difference but the degree of difference he perceived.

COMPATIBILITY OF BACKGROUND

The pets marked above may have been a dog and a cat. Another person might have said to himself, "A dog and a cat aren't all that different. Both are small, are kept in the house, and require essentially the same kinds of food and grooming." That person might have put the X much farther to the left. If, on the other hand, the person once had a snake as a pet and his beloved a llama, he would have put the X where it is shown above.

The point is this: an X on these continuums indicates difference—and how much difference is perceived or felt. If you do not perceive that the difference is great, you will put your X much closer to the share side of the continuum. If you think the difference is significant, put your X closer to the do not share side of the continuum.

The quiz for each person is different—on one, the share side is to the right, and on the other, the share side is to the left. Again, mark your forms independently of each other, and rely on your first impulse. Don't spend too much time thinking about one response.

BACKGROUND COMPATIBILITY QUIZ

PERSON A

If you believe you and your beloved shared an identical or extremely similar background in a particular area, put your X close to the left side of the continuum. If you did not share a similar background, put your X toward the right. The farther to the right, the more the difference you see in the two backgrounds.

	We share the same	**We do not share the same**
race		
tribe		
language		
family structure		
cultural customs		
nationality		
religion		
denomination		
social class		
economic background		
childhood privileges		
education		
travel experience		
number of close friends		
feelings toward our parents of the same sex		
feelings toward our parents of the opposite sex		
feelings toward our older siblings		
feelings toward our younger siblings		
feelings toward our aunts and uncles		
feelings toward our friends		
feelings toward our past lives		

BACKGROUND COMPATIBILITY QUIZ

PERSON B

If you believe you and your beloved shared an identical or extremely similar background in a particular area, put your X close to the right side of the continuum. If you did not share a similar background, put your X toward the left. The farther to the left, the more the difference you see in the two backgrounds.

	We do not share the same					We share the same			
race									
tribe									
language									
family structure									
cultural customs									
nationality									
religion									
denomination									
social class									
economic background									
childhood privileges									
education									
travel experience									
number of close friends									
feelings toward our parents of the same sex									
feelings toward our parents of the opposite sex									
feelings toward our older siblings									
feelings toward our younger siblings									
feelings toward our aunts and uncles									
feelings toward our friends									
feelings toward our past lives									

ARE WE COMPATIBLE?

Evaluating Your Responses

Transfer your responses to the third form, "Your Background Compatibility as a Couple." The dotted line down the middle of the form is the share position for both quizzes. Transfer the marks made by *Person A to the right of the dotted line* and the marks made by *Person B to the left of the dotted line.* Then connect the positions in a vertical fashion as shown on the samples below:

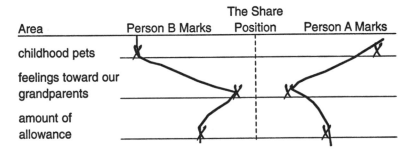

Area	Person B Marks	The Share Position	Person A Marks
childhood pets			
feelings toward our grandparents			
amount of allowance			

After you have connected the marks, go back to chapter 2 and take a look at "Compatibility Model A." The gaps in the responses on the form create a similar pattern.

These gaps reflect your perceptions of your differences as well as your differences. They reflect opinions as well as reality. Are you and your beloved wide apart in many areas? Then work is required to bring about agreement.

Delight in areas of natural compatibility (that is, areas that are very close to the center line).

Compatibility of background is an important area of compatibility. Being exactly alike, however, is not as important as the ways in which you and your beloved perceive the differences.

YOUR BACKGROUND COMPATIBILITY
AS A COUPLE

Transfer both sets of responses to this form. The marks for Person A go to the right of the dotted line, regarding the dotted line as the share position on the previous form. The marks for Person B go to the left of the dotted line, again regarding the dotted line as the share position.

Area	Person B Marks	The Share Position	Person A Marks
race			
tribe			
language			
family structure			
cultural customs			
nationality			
religion			
denomination			
social class			
economic background			
childhood privileges			
education			
travel experience			
number of close friends			
feelings toward our parents of the same sex			
feelings toward our parents of the opposite sex			
feelings toward our older siblings			
feelings toward our younger siblings			
feelings toward our aunts and uncles			
feelings toward our friends			
feelings toward our past lives			

ARE WE COMPATIBLE?

One of the best marriages I've ever witnessed is that of Daren and Denise. Denise is Caucasian, from Nebraska, and was raised on a farm. Daren is Negro, from Jamaica, and was raised in a city. Both were raised in staunch English-culture homes—with exquisite manners, a great love of literature and music, loving families, and a nearly identical set of values. They had very similar childhood experiences, without major tragedies or difficulties. Their cultures were very much alike, as were their family structures, their circle of friends, and their educational backgrounds. They regarded their obvious racial difference in background as being, in Daren's terms, "only as thick as a few cells of pigment."

To an outsider, their differences might have seemed obvious and great. They had a tremendous amount of natural harmony, however, and over the twenty years of their marriage, they have had extremely few conflicts regarding their backgrounds.

Background differences can be bridged if both parties are willing to make the effort to do so, and if past tragedies have been dealt with in a healthy manner. Never assume that the past doesn't matter. Never assume that the past is in the past. The past does matter, and it does affect the present and future of the relationship. Be open with each other about the past. Explore the differences fully. And include in your planning for marriage how your agreements might extend to your family members and friends.

Chapter 6

EMOTIONAL COMPATIBILITY

Temperament is the one area in which opposites frequently attract. For example, the hotheaded person may find the coolheaded person to be safe and comfortable. The coolheaded person may find the hotheaded person to be passionate and exciting. Or the outgoing person may find the shy person someone to cherish and protect, while the shy person finds the outgoing person someone who is fun and refreshing.

Though opposites attract, they are far more difficult to bind together than two people of similar temperament. Over time, opposite personality traits tend to gnaw away at compatibility.

That's what happened in the case of Dan and Nicole. When Dan came into my office, he slumped into the sofa and sighed deeply before he ever said a word. "Everything

ARE WE COMPATIBLE?

with her is high drama, at the extremes, out there. Nothing is ever easy or smooth flowing. There's always got to be some intense emotion. In fact, if there isn't, she's not happy."

Dan initially had been attracted to Nicole, who was an art major, by her intensity and her artistic flair. I asked Dan how he thought Nicole regarded him. "As a bore," he said. "She claims that I have no passion and that I don't really care about anything to the point of fighting for it. She may be partly right. But I just need a rest."

Dan and Nicole stayed together and eventually married. Through a series of counseling sessions, they came to appreciate their differences and also to see the need for an agreement that included lots of space and time-outs.

They agreed that they found each other more interesting if they didn't spend all of their free time together. They even took separate vacations. Dan went on hiking trips alone or with male friends. Nicole once went to a spa and, on another occasion, took a cruise—each time traveling with another woman.

The differences and variances in personality are far too numerous to explore fully in one section of a book. We inevitably must draw fairly broad conclusions. One is that in most relationships, differences make for excitement, variety, and intrigue. Another is that similarities make for stability and balance.

Concern should arise when a couple find that they have mostly differences, that their similarities are not positive ones, or that they are unable to bridge their differences with agreement.

EMOTIONAL COMPATIBILITY

Two people who perceive themselves to be vastly different in temperament can anticipate a rocky road—one full of arguments and surprises, some of which may be pleasant and others unpleasant. The important agreement they must reach is to resolve arguments peaceably and to work through their surprises with a sense of personal balance.

Be wary of similarities that are not positive character traits—for example, if both people seem prone toward anger, melancholy, despair, depression, or addiction.

Six traits are vital to emotional compatibility, and we'll explore each in turn: (1) the ability to "fight fair" and resolve conflicts, (2) flexibility, (3) generosity, (4) a sense of humor, (5) courtesy, and (6) self-assurance.

Trait Number 1: Fighting Fair and Resolving Conflicts

Differences of opinion arise in every relationship. If the differences are great, or the feelings associated with them are fairly intense, an argument results.

There's always an element of power play in an argument. Be wary, however, if one person always insists on winning or having things go his or her way. That pattern inevitably tears away at compatibility.

Also be concerned if you never have disagreements with your beloved. Ask yourself, Why not? You have differences. What keeps them from surfacing? Are you afraid to disagree? Is one person submissive to the point of silence?

How do you decide where to go on a date? Does one person always make the decision? What if you want to go out for pizza and your beloved wants a hamburger? What happens if you want to see different movies or listen to different radio stations? How do you resolve these fairly routine, minor differences?

Several things are necessary for a disagreement truly to be a fair fight:

- No idle threats should be made. No ultimatums should be associated with the outcome of the argument.
- No physical violence should be used.
- The more intense the feelings, the greater is the need for a cooling off period before the issue is discussed.
- Both parties must stick to the present issue—no bringing up the past.
- Avoid personal attack—that is, direct references to the person's physical appearance, background, personality, or any other ingrained, inherent, or deep-seated trait. No insults. No name-calling.
- Avoid absolute statements, such as *always* and *never*.

And After the Fight?

What happens after you and your beloved quarrel? Are you able to resume closeness? Are you able to move forward in your relationship?

Fair fights should result in compromise that makes for greater consistency and predictability in a relationship. The relationship should be strengthened after you and your beloved have weathered a squall. If your beloved walks away from disagreements in a huff, only to stew in silence for prolonged periods, the argument isn't truly over at that point. It's only brewing for later eruption.

Trait Number 2: Flexibility

Flexibility is the ability to go with the flow—to change directions or make new plans almost on a moment's notice. Flexibility is vital to a marriage.

Scheduling Flexibility

It's inevitable that you and your beloved are occasionally going to be detained against your wills—whether owing to a tie-up in traffic, a broken elevator, or an unexpected call from a supervisor. Are both able to accommodate those delays? How about no-shows, canceled events, or the need to move appointments from one date to another?

Flexibility in Making Choices

We often don't get our first choice. The supply has run out. The flight is already booked. The table is already reserved. The decision has been made by someone with greater authority. Are both of you able to handle those situations and move immediately to plan B or another option?

One thing to which both must be committed, however, is this: once you have exercised an option, including your option to marry each other, both must be willing to embrace that decision fully and be satisfied with it.

Crisis-Related Flexibility

Trouble happens, regardless of the person or couple. Children get sick. Cars get dinged. Water pipes leak. Companies cut back their staffs. Human beings fail other human beings.

Take a look at the way each has faced crises in the past.

Does your beloved have a tendency to run and hide, give up, or collapse? Or does your beloved tend to duck, dodge, and cope and, when the crisis has passed, emerge standing tall and strong?

Trait Number 3: Generosity

Generosity is expansive. It gives. It grows. In a marriage, generosity can be considered love in action. It covers a multitude of errors, and it provides an atmosphere rich in these qualities: the ability to give, forgive, and let live.

Giving

The generous person gives not only in material ways but in time, a listening ear, and warm embraces. The giving person is not stingy with self or things.

If both partners in a marriage are generous to each other, yet maintain that generosity within the bounds of budgets, common courtesy, and without manipulative motives, the generous marriage can be a most comforting and delightful relationship.

You need to remind yourself daily to give to your spouse as you gave when you were first dating. Give the following:

- Compliments
- Little kisses
- Applause
- A word of encouragement
- An embrace
- Nice surprises

EMOTIONAL COMPATIBILITY

Generosity includes availability. Be available to listen, to help meet a need. Don't withhold physical intimacy.

Ask yourselves as you prepare for marriage, Are we generous with each other? Are we creative in our means of giving to each other? Do we require that we receive before we give? Is one of us keeping score in the relationship, or is the balance in our mutual giving a natural one?

Some people have a great need to receive. They require a great deal of attention, a great many gifts, a great host of compliments. This need can be a sign of low self-esteem. A person with healthy self-esteem and confidence does not need an abundance of gifts to feel good about himself or herself.

Others feel that the beloved one constantly needs more than they can give. In some cases, the person who is perceived as needy isn't needy at all. It's more a matter that the person who feels compelled to give has nothing to give! Take a look at your capacity to give. Do you *want* to give to your future spouse? How much? In what ways? How often?

Still others give primarily with a goal of receiving. This, at its heart, is manipulative. True giving is done without anticipating a return.

Forgiving

A second hallmark of generosity is the ability to forgive freely and frequently. Forgiving is letting go. It means not holding grudges, not seeking revenge, not exacting justice, not demanding retribution.

Confrontation is necessary at times. Confrontation permits a person to express the feeling of being wronged, cheated, rejected, or hurt. Confrontation is healthy in a relationship. What happens after confrontation is the critical factor.

When confronted, are both you and your beloved willing to weigh the claims in a calm, reasonable manner? Are both willing to talk out differences of opinion? Do you admit when you are wrong? Are you sorry when you realize that you have hurt the other person? Do you make an extra effort to change your offending ways so that you do not hurt the person in the future?

Be wary if you discover that your beloved is holding deep-seated hatred against another person or group of people. That same propensity toward hatred and anger can be turned toward you.

An Ability to "Live and Let Live"

Generosity is also marked by a willingness to "let live." The generous person allows others personal space and freedom to make their own mistakes.

When Gene came to speak to me, I could tell by his body language that he was tied in knots. He immediately folded his legs and arms and scrunched over in his seat. "I can't breathe," he said.

"I'm sure of that," I noted. "Try standing up, raising your hands, and stretching." He laughed and did as I suggested, then sat down in a more relaxed manner.

"Carol is smothering me," he said. "She wants to know everywhere I go, every person I talk to, every word that is said, everything that is done. If I don't tell her, she clams up. Last night when I went over to her apartment, I found her crying. She insisted that I am cheating on her. No proof—

just a hunch she had. She refused to go out with me, refused to let me try to talk sense to her. I can't tell if she's jealous, controlling, or just crazy."

"She's probably none of the above," I assured him. "She's probably insecure. Insecure people have a very difficult time in giving, forgiving, or allowing others the opportunity to live their own lives."

"What can I do to make her feel more secure?"

"You can be consistent, over time. You can model behavior that gives, forgives, and lets live. But, Gene, you can't *make* her feel secure. You're going to have to decide if you can wait for Carol to come to the place where she is secure in herself and in her relationship with you."

Gene continued to date Carol for two more years. Finally, he broke off their relationship. Carol dated two more men before she married, and her marriage lasted only a few months. The break-ups have no doubt only added to her insecurity.

A close cousin of insecurity is jealousy. A jealous person believes that someone else has what is rightfully his or hers. Jealousy in small doses can be a healthy emotion. Only when a person perceives that someone else has something that is rightfully hers—and in reality, the person doesn't—is jealousy misdirected and unhealthy. A woman, for example, can be jealous that another woman is about to go on a business trip with her husband. If her husband has a track record of being faithful to her, however, there is no reason for her to allow jealousy to build.

Ask yourselves, Do we trust each other? Is either one excessively jealous? Are we suspicious of each other's motives or behaviors? Do we give each other sufficient space to grow? If your beloved can't stand to have you out of sight, be wary.

Trait Number 4: A Sense of Humor

A sense of humor is like a big dose of joy in a marriage. How wonderful to be able to laugh at what truly is humorous in life—the foibles and goofs that are natural and normal! How grand to see the lighter side of life and appreciate it!

A sense of humor is *not* rooted in ridicule or cynicism. Its base is mutual fun. If one person doesn't think something is funny, it isn't. If one person doesn't want to be teased, the person shouldn't be.

Ask yourselves, Do we laugh at the same jokes? Can we make each other laugh? Do we tease in a way that isn't hurtful to each other? Is the humor we share rooted in cynicism, or is it drawn from life's innocent mistakes and human foibles? Do we have an ability to laugh at ourselves, both as individuals and as a couple?

Pay particular attention to this last question. Are you able to laugh at your innocent mistakes or embarrassing moments? Can your beloved laugh at his or her foibles and quirks? If so, you probably have a good basis for being able to laugh at some of your unique oddities as a couple, including some of your seeming incompatibilities.

The dour person who never laughs is probably not going to be much fun to live with. Be concerned if your beloved sees no humor in life. He or she isn't seeing all of life from a healthy perspective.

Trait Number 5: Courtesy

Common courtesy isn't all that common these days! *Courtesy* is another word for manners, which are a manifestation of respect.

Do you and your beloved treat each other with respect? Do you extend to each other the same degree of manners that you would extend to a person you considered to be famous, important, or powerful?

Courtesy includes saying please and thank you. It means not invading a person's privacy. It means not interrupting in conversations to correct a would-be error unless vital information is being incorrectly stated.

A discourteous person projects the impression: "I don't need to be kind to you." That implies possession or control. Courteous behavior sends a different message: "I'm still courting you. I'm still trying to show you how much I respect you and value you."

Trait Number 6: Self-Assurance

Self-assurance is not the same as self-reliance. The self-reliant person says, "I can live my life on my own, and I don't need anybody's help." The self-assured person, by contrast, says, "I can survive on my own if I have to, but I prefer to live in mutually beneficial relationships with others."

The self-assured person is confident and has healthy self-esteem, not demanding that others do for her what she is capable of doing on her own. At the same time, a person

ARE WE COMPATIBLE?

who truly feels deep inner assurance about life is generally more willing to take risks, be vulnerable, and reach out to others.

Most of us gravitate toward others who have strengths that we don't have. We find comfort in their abilities, knowledge, or experience. A danger arises when one person is perceived as having *all* of the strengths, the other all of the weaknesses.

If the weak person doesn't choose to become strong, he tends over time to become more reliant on the strength of the other person, not less reliant. The end result of this unhealthy process is that the weak person never discovers his potential for strength. Eventually, the strong person may feel depleted, unable to carry the emotional, intellectual, or physical load of two lives. At that point, a marriage can crumble quickly.

Be wary of the person who believes he or she has no strengths. Be equally wary of a person who admits to no weaknesses. The healthy person will recognize that he or she is a mixture of strengths and weaknesses. In harmonious compatibility, one person's strengths will match another's weaknesses.

If two people are strong in one area, they seem to be more than doubly strong as a couple in that area. There's a multiplication in their shared strength.

If the two people are weak in the same areas, their combined weakness is something they need to recognize and seek to strengthen through outside help.

Ask yourselves as you prepare for marriage, Are we willing to admit our weaknesses and acknowledge our strengths?

EMOTIONAL COMPATIBILITY

Can we talk openly about our weaknesses and strengths with each other? Is one of us strong where the other is weak? Do we help each other in these areas? Are there areas in which we both feel weak? How might we become stronger in these areas? Are there areas in which we both are strong? How might we learn to combine our strengths so as to help other individuals or couples in this area?

Evaluating Your Emotional Speed and Space

Two other general areas of emotional compatibility are worthy of note. I find it helpful to think of them in terms of emotional speed and the need for emotional space. Ask yourselves, How quickly does each of us respond emotionally to a situation? How much privacy and distance does each need in responding emotionally or resolving emotional issues?

Emotional Response Time

We all know people who are quick-tempered or those who say about their anger, "I flare quickly and then I'm over it." These people respond emotionally with great speed. Others operate at a slow burn, and their emotions build to a full climax, which may eventually be just as intense but take much more time for expression. Still others feel and express emotions quickly, but then hold on to the emotions for a long time. Some let their emotions build, but once they've expressed them, they are able to let go of the emotions and move on.

In some counseling sessions I ask individuals or couples to

ARE WE COMPATIBLE?

draw their emotional response patterns to life. A few of them are shown below:

Tammy

Norman

Dirk

Penny

You can almost feel the energy in these drawings. Note especially Penny's drawing. She interpreted this to me as a reluctance to let go of emotions or situations. She said, "I always seem to be revisiting the same issues, the same feelings."

A difference in the speed of emotional response can have a great impact on a marriage.

Dot and Karl had different patterns of emotional response. Dot was very easygoing. She rarely expressed herself with intense emotions; she was not prone to belly laughs, crying jags, or deep sighs. Karl, by contrast, was an emotional roulette wheel. His big gusto laugh could be followed almost immediately by raging anger or by withdrawn silence. Karl could move through a wide range of emotions in one day.

Because they lived in cities twenty miles apart, they dated only a short time prior to their engagement, and their dates tended to be only three or four hours long. Dot rarely saw more than one emotion in Karl during an evening together.

EMOTIONAL COMPATIBILITY

Shortly before they were to be married, Dot moved into the same apartment building where Karl lived (occupying their future two-bedroom home). She saw Karl several times a day, and what she saw frightened her and wore her out emotionally. The man who came to her door at 8:00 A.M. and drove her to work often did not seem to be the same person she met for lunch or the same person who drove her home. Yet another emotion might be omnipresent in Karl when they had dinner together, or when he came over later in the evening to watch television. She said to me, "I never knew which Karl was going to walk through the door." She broke off their engagement two weeks prior to their wedding and moved five hundred miles away.

Emotional Tension

Although we may not be able to change our basic temperament, we must recognize that we can change the way in which we express our emotions. We can

- lower the volume of our voices.
- change the object of our harangues to something inanimate.
- identify and express emotions before they build to the point of eruption.
- seek physical means of working off the excess stress we feel.
- wail, weep, and gnash our teeth alone.

In many cases, we need to give our partners space—recognizing that they don't need to hear us roar, feel the full force of our emotional outbursts, or be our emotional punching bags.

Regardless of your emotional responses to life, when you are in relationship with another person, you must take into consideration his or her ability to receive and respond to your emotional expressions. This is not to say that you need to stifle your emotions or become emotionally inhibited (if you tend to be overly expressive), nor do you need to generate emotions or become emotionally uninhibited (if you tend to be underexpressive). Be free to express yourself genuinely and openly. But if you are expressing yourself in the presence of your beloved or any other person, and you want a positive response from that person, you must communicate your emotions in a way that is acceptable to him or her.

Ask yourselves, Do we feel free to express ourselves emotionally to each other? Is each comfortable with the way the other expresses himself or herself emotionally? What might we need to change so that each person feels more comfortable and is better able to respond?

Emotional Space

Some people like to be left alone to work out their ideas, feelings, and responses to life in private. Others have a great need to talk out all their feelings.

Again, both ways of coping are normal and acceptable. Within a marriage, incompatibility arises when one person forces his or her means of response on the other in a way that is uncomfortable for that person.

If both people are talkers, the marriage tends to be highly verbal, with lots of emotional analysis and expression.

EMOTIONAL COMPATIBILITY

If both people are loners, the marriage can be a quiet relationship that is likely to be quite satisfying, especially if both are able to communicate periodically about what they are going through in their respective inner worlds.

If one person is a talker and the other is a loner, there's a natural incompatibility. Talkers tend to be very frustrated that the loners they love are unable to talk about their emotions freely or to accommodate the emotions they express. Loners tend to be overwhelmed by the emotions of the talkers they love, and they tend to regard those emotions as being more superficial because they are expressed so often.

Teresa was a talker, and Justin was a loner. Teresa had a great need to express how she was feeling at any particular moment. Justin responded, "I'm not sure I even know how to feel some of the emotions she talks about."

Justin wasn't used to labeling his feelings or talking about them, and such conversations with Teresa were uncomfortable. He preferred to come to conclusions about life, including his emotional response, alone and over time. Once Justin had come to a conclusion, however, he tended to be stable in it.

Teresa told Justin that she loved him at the end of their first date—and meant it. Justin thought she was joking. He viewed her subsequent expressions of "I love you" as surface-level feelings, not true expressions of her heart. Teresa had fallen madly in love within hours, and what she felt, she genuinely felt. Justin didn't arrive at the conclusion that he loved Teresa until after they had dated for ten months—during which time Teresa thought there was no hope that Justin would ever love her in return.

ARE WE COMPATIBLE?

In time, Teresa recognized that she needed to give Justin space and time to work out his feelings. And Justin came to realize that Teresa's spontaneous responses to life were genuinely the way she felt.

If a talker is unable to find satisfaction in communicating emotions to a loner mate, both partners in the relationship need to come to some form of agreement that allows the talker to express feelings. At times, the talker may need to find a neutral third party who has a willing ear, is capable of keeping a confidence, and has no emotional investment in the marriage. A better solution, perhaps, is for the loner to allow the talker full expression of emotions within limited time frames.

Ask yourselves as you contemplate getting married, Are there times when each needs more space in order to sort out feelings? Are there times when one of us needs for the other to be more communicative about feelings so that where he or she stands in the relationship is clear? Can we talk to each other about the emotional space we need?

Intense emotions can be smothering to the person who tends to respond to life more intellectually, physically, or spiritually and less emotionally. A lack of expressed emotion can be bewildering or appear as a void to the person who responds to life with deep emotions.

If you and your beloved aren't on the same wavelength emotionally, recognize the differences and seek some means of tuning each other in. How each person feels, and how each person expresses feelings, is a big part of any marriage relationship. Compatibility of feelings is not necessary, and neither is compatibility in the way a person expresses feelings in private. But compatibility in the way each person expresses emotion to the other person in the marriage *is* important.

An Emotional Temperament Quiz

We rarely see ourselves clearly when it comes to our emotional temperaments. For that reason, the "Emotional Temperament Quiz" is based on how you feel about yourself and on how you regard the other person in the relationship. Each of you will fill out two forms—one for yourself, and the other for your beloved.

On the quiz forms, you will respond to a series of continuums that reflect opposite emotions. Here is an example:

```
I am                    X                        I am
introverted  +--+--+--+--+--+--+--+--+--+  extroverted
```

If you believe that the vast majority of your statements are positive—whether about the weather, your beloved, the condition of the world, or your latest experience—you would put your X where it is shown above on the form labeled "I am . . . ." If you recognize that your talk is highly peppered with criticism, negative comments, or sarcasm, your mark would go toward the other end of the continuum.

On the form labeled "My beloved is . . ." put your marks where you think your beloved's most common responses will fall.

EMOTIONAL TEMPERAMENT QUIZ

PERSON A

On the form below, mark responses about yourself.

I am . . .

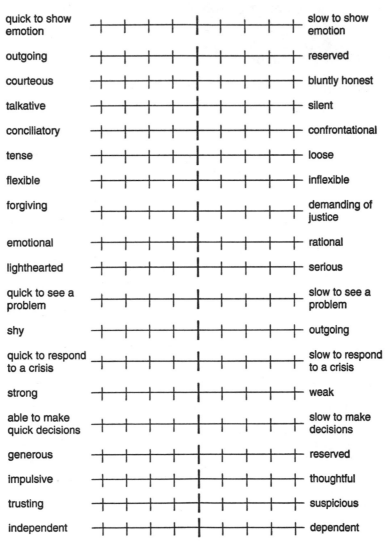

quick to show emotion	slow to show emotion
outgoing	reserved
courteous	bluntly honest
talkative	silent
conciliatory	confrontational
tense	loose
flexible	inflexible
forgiving	demanding of justice
emotional	rational
lighthearted	serious
quick to see a problem	slow to see a problem
shy	outgoing
quick to respond to a crisis	slow to respond to a crisis
strong	weak
able to make quick decisions	slow to make decisions
generous	reserved
impulsive	thoughtful
trusting	suspicious
independent	dependent

On the form below, mark responses about your beloved.

My beloved is . . .

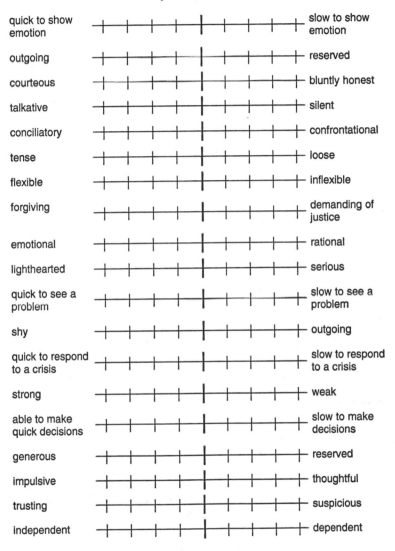

quick to show emotion	slow to show emotion
outgoing	reserved
courteous	bluntly honest
talkative	silent
conciliatory	confrontational
tense	loose
flexible	inflexible
forgiving	demanding of justice
emotional	rational
lighthearted	serious
quick to see a problem	slow to see a problem
shy	outgoing
quick to respond to a crisis	slow to respond to a crisis
strong	weak
able to make quick decisions	slow to make decisions
generous	reserved
impulsive	thoughtful
trusting	suspicious
independent	dependent

EMOTIONAL TEMPERAMENT QUIZ

PERSON B

On the form below, mark responses about yourself.

I am . . .

quick to show emotion	——┼——┼——┼——┼——╋——┼——┼——┼——┼——	slow to show emotion
outgoing	——┼——┼——┼——┼——╋——┼——┼——┼——┼——	reserved
courteous	——┼——┼——┼——┼——╋——┼——┼——┼——┼——	bluntly honest
talkative	——┼——┼——┼——┼——╋——┼——┼——┼——┼——	silent
conciliatory	——┼——┼——┼——┼——╋——┼——┼——┼——┼——	confrontational
tense	——┼——┼——┼——┼——╋——┼——┼——┼——┼——	loose
flexible	——┼——┼——┼——┼——╋——┼——┼——┼——┼——	inflexible
forgiving	——┼——┼——┼——┼——╋——┼——┼——┼——┼——	demanding of justice
emotional	——┼——┼——┼——┼——╋——┼——┼——┼——┼——	rational
lighthearted	——┼——┼——┼——┼——╋——┼——┼——┼——┼——	serious
quick to see a problem	——┼——┼——┼——┼——╋——┼——┼——┼——┼——	slow to see a problem
shy	——┼——┼——┼——┼——╋——┼——┼——┼——┼——	outgoing
quick to respond to a crisis	——┼——┼——┼——┼——╋——┼——┼——┼——┼——	slow to respond to a crisis
strong	——┼——┼——┼——┼——╋——┼——┼——┼——┼——	weak
able to make quick decisions	——┼——┼——┼——┼——╋——┼——┼——┼——┼——	slow to make decisions
generous	——┼——┼——┼——┼——╋——┼——┼——┼——┼——	reserved
impulsive	——┼——┼——┼——┼——╋——┼——┼——┼——┼——	thoughtful
trusting	——┼——┼——┼——┼——╋——┼——┼——┼——┼——	suspicious
independent	——┼——┼——┼——┼——╋——┼——┼——┼——┼——	dependent

On the form below, mark responses about your beloved.

My beloved is . . .

quick to show emotion		slow to show emotion
outgoing		reserved
courteous		bluntly honest
talkative		silent
conciliatory		confrontational
tense		loose
flexible		inflexible
forgiving		demanding of justice
emotional		rational
lighthearted		serious
quick to see a problem		slow to see a problem
shy		outgoing
quick to respond to a crisis		slow to respond to a crisis
strong		weak
able to make quick decisions		slow to make decisions
generous		reserved
impulsive		thoughtful
trusting		suspicious
independent		dependent

ARE WE COMPATIBLE?

As with all of the forms, but especially so with this one, you are likely to squelch your responses, not wanting to hurt your beloved. You also will have the tendency to skew your responses toward a more positive or negative position, depending on whether you tend to have high or low self-esteem. For this form to have validity, and for you and your beloved to begin to forge agreements in areas of natural incompatibility, each needs to be *extremely* honest with the other and with oneself. As with the previous quizzes, go with your first response.

Make a pact with each other in advance of completing these forms that you are going to be truthful, and that you expect something positive to come from this quiz that will strengthen your relationship and help each of you reach more of individual potential.

Evaluating Your Responses

First, match up your responses so that you are taking a look at "She said about herself and I said about her" and "He said about himself and I said about him." You can make the comparisons verbally or visually by laying the two forms side by side, or you can combine the responses to one form.

Talk candidly with each other about each discrepancy. Talk about how you feel, not whether the person is right or wrong. Whenever possible, affirm that you like the response that your beloved has given.

One person may become defensive. If that happens, recognize that it is happening! Don't accuse each other. Do give each other sufficient time and space to think about what both have noted on the forms.

EMOTIONAL COMPATIBILITY

Ask God to give both of you discernment and wisdom, and to cause a new and deeper level of love to grow between you as you confront your personal strengths and weaknesses and, in so doing, confront your strengths and weaknesses as a couple.

Do not part in anger over this conversation. Go into your discussion with a firm resolve that you will find a means of ending your conversation on a positive note.

An Emotional Compatibility Quiz

After you have discussed your responses to the "Emotional Temperament Quiz," you are ready to take the "Emotional Compatibility Quiz." Each person responds on a separate form.

On this quiz, you will respond to the conversation you have just had about emotional temperaments. You will note how you felt prior to, during, and after the conversation, and you will mark some summary statements about the conversation.

EMOTIONAL COMPATIBILITY QUIZ

PERSON A

On the form below, mark the way you feel about the conversation that you have had regarding your respective emotional temperaments.

Before our conversation, I felt . . .

uptight	—┼—┼—┼—┼—╋—┼—┼—┼—┼—	relaxed
eager	—┼—┼—┼—┼—╋—┼—┼—┼—┼—	hesitant
courageous	—┼—┼—┼—┼—╋—┼—┼—┼—┼—	fearful
open	—┼—┼—┼—┼—╋—┼—┼—┼—┼—	closed
unwilling	—┼—┼—┼—┼—╋—┼—┼—┼—┼—	willing

During our conversation, I felt . . .

awkward	—┼—┼—┼—┼—╋—┼—┼—┼—┼—	at ease
emotional	—┼—┼—┼—┼—╋—┼—┼—┼—┼—	rational
threatened	—┼—┼—┼—┼—╋—┼—┼—┼—┼—	comforted
aggressive	—┼—┼—┼—┼—╋—┼—┼—┼—┼—	passive
strong	—┼—┼—┼—┼—╋—┼—┼—┼—┼—	weak
comfortable	—┼—┼—┼—┼—╋—┼—┼—┼—┼—	uncomfortable
limited	—┼—┼—┼—┼—╋—┼—┼—┼—┼—	unlimited

As the result of our conversation, I felt . . .

assaulted	—┼—┼—┼—┼—╋—┼—┼—┼—┼—	reassured
peaceful	—┼—┼—┼—┼—╋—┼—┼—┼—┼—	in turmoil
hurt	—┼—┼—┼—┼—╋—┼—┼—┼—┼—	loved
helped	—┼—┼—┼—┼—╋—┼—┼—┼—┼—	wounded
better	—┼—┼—┼—┼—╋—┼—┼—┼—┼—	worse

EMOTIONAL COMPATIBILITY QUIZ

PERSON B

On the form below, mark the way you feel about the conversation that you have had regarding your respective emotional temperaments.

Before our conversation, I felt . . .

uptight		relaxed
eager		hesitant
courageous		fearful
open		closed
unwilling		willing

During our conversation, I felt . . .

awkward		at ease
emotional		rational
threatened		comforted
aggressive		passive
strong		weak
comfortable		uncomfortable
limited		unlimited

As the result of our conversation, I felt . . .

assaulted		reassured
peaceful		in turmoil
hurt		loved
helped		wounded
better		worse

ARE WE COMPATIBLE?

Evaluating Your Responses

Transfer both sets of marks to the form "Your Emotional Compatibility as a Couple." Do not be concerned about which marks belong to which person. Draw vertical lines to connect the points as shown below.

Before our conversation, we felt . . .

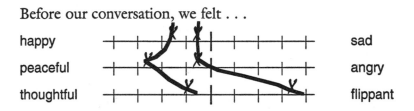

happy		sad
peaceful		angry
thoughtful		flippant

Take a look at the gaps between responses. These responses reflect the way in which each felt comfortable with the process of talking about emotions or in showing emotion to the other. This quiz, not the one regarding your temperaments, is the measure of your emotional *compatibility*.

Where do your greatest differences lie? What might you do to bridge the differences?

If one or both of you were unwilling to complete the "Emotional Temperament Quiz," if you were not able to discuss your emotional temperaments and the responses to the quiz, or if one or both of you were unwilling to complete the "Emotional Compatibility Quiz," be concerned. As a couple, you are not willing to express your true selves or your true opinions of each other to each other. You definitely have a communication problem, and you may very well have an emotional incompatibility that one or both of you may sense but be unwilling to express.

YOUR EMOTIONAL COMPATIBILITY AS A COUPLE

Transfer both sets of responses to the "Emotional Compatibility Quiz" to this form. Do not pay attention to which person made which mark. Connect the responses vertically to reveal the gaps more clearly.

Before our conversation, we felt . . .

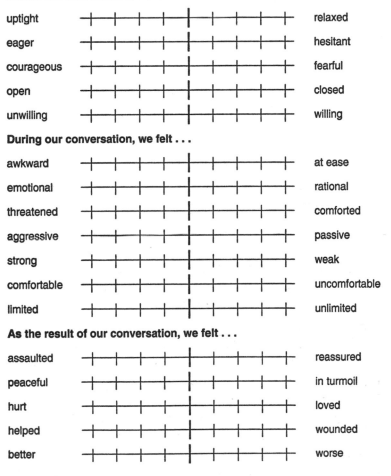

uptight	relaxed
eager	hesitant
courageous	fearful
open	closed
unwilling	willing

During our conversation, we felt . . .

awkward	at ease
emotional	rational
threatened	comforted
aggressive	passive
strong	weak
comfortable	uncomfortable
limited	unlimited

As the result of our conversation, we felt . . .

assaulted	reassured
peaceful	in turmoil
hurt	loved
helped	wounded
better	worse

ARE WE COMPATIBLE?

No emotions are bad or invalid. Nevertheless, the expression of emotions may be seen as appropriate or inappropriate, beneficial or harmful and, thus, positive or negative. The expression of emotions is important to compatibility far more than the emotions themselves. If you and your beloved can agree on how to effectively and positively communicate emotions to each other, compatibility can be forged even if, by temperament, there is no natural harmony.

Chapter 7

COMPATIBILITY OF GOALS AND DREAMS

Perhaps the easiest compatibility to recognize is that related to goals and dreams. Most people tend to be fairly open and honest in expressing what they want out of life. I find that many couples talk openly about their goals and dreams related to marriage, children, careers, and future finances very early in their dating relationships.

Goals tend to cluster into three main categories: (1) marriage and children, (2) work (or career) and its rewards, and (3) memberships and associations.

The Terms

Before we discuss these categories, it may be helpful to take a look at several terms that are sometimes used interchangeably by couples anticipating marriage—terms that actually define very different states of being or processes.

The Nature of Goals

For a goal truly to be a goal, it must be achievable. Goals need to be firmly rooted in reality.

Goals generally are reached through committed effort. They don't just happen on their own accord.

When marriage partners set a goal, both persons must be mutually committed to make the necessary effort to achieving that goal. "A good marriage" cannot be the goal of just one person in the marriage. Some goals are personal and achievable on an individual basis. But the goal of a good marriage is not one of them.

A dream, as contrasted to a goal, is something that you hope and believe will happen as the result of your best efforts but not something that can be guaranteed. A dream might be stated as a hope or as a faith statement. I can say today that I dream of being healthy as a ninety-two-year-old person. I can set this as a goal to which I devote committed effort. It is an achievable goal, given the average life expectancy of my forefathers. But being in good health at ninety-two is nothing that anybody can guarantee. It is a dream.

Dream Elements

Most goals have an element of dream in them, which is why they are lumped together here. We are such a goal-oriented, achievement-oriented society, however, we often lose sight of the fact that to a certain degree, we are never the masters of our own destinies.

COMPATIBILITY OF GOALS AND DREAMS

Tony and Alice had a goal of having four children. After they were married, Alice was diagnosed as having a congenital condition that made it impossible for her to conceive. Their dream of children was shattered overnight. They had never thought of their goal as having a dream element. They simply assumed that they would be able to bear children and that they would have four children. As it turned out, they adopted twins.

Goals were adjusted and reset when their dreams did not turn into reality. And that's the most important aspect of goals and dreams as they affect compatibility: Are both of you able to adjust goals and dreams to life's reality?

Marriage and Children

"How many kids would you like to have someday?" Couples often talk about what kind of parents they hope to be, and once they are seriously talking about marriage to each other, what kind of parent each hopes the other will be to the children.

Far less common are discussions related to these questions: What do I expect of myself as a spouse—what do I intend to do for my spouse? What do I expect my spouse to do for me?

Tad and Stefanie had very different expectations about the spouses they wanted and wanted to be. Tad wanted a wife who would stay at home, keep a clean house, have dinner waiting for him when he came home, and take care of the family checkbook. He envisioned his future bride as someone who would wisely spend his money for their mutual benefit, be a good cook, and support him in the decisions he made. What did Stefanie expect? She expected Tad to take her out to eat often, to buy her lovely gifts, and to do at least half the housework.

Their expectations about each other were not totally unfounded. Every time Tad came to Stefanie's apartment, it was clean. She had invited him over several times to delicious dinners. Her bank account was in good order. From Stefanie's perspective, Tad had been very generous in taking her out to eat and buying her presents, and she appreciated his offers to empty the trash and help load the dishwasher when he came over to dinner.

Neither had voiced expectations about what Tad intended to do as a *husband* and Stefanie intended to do as a *wife*. Such expectations need to be practical. Tad, had he voiced his expectations, might very well have said that he expected to work from eight to six every day, turn his paychecks over to Stefanie for wise management, and take Stefanie out on Saturday nights to movies or dinner. Stefanie might have said that she expected to shop a lot and clean house a little.

Neither one expected to do laundry, shop for groceries, cook meals, vacuum, dust, mop, wash dishes, empty trash, make beds, iron clothes, balance the checkbook, mow the lawn, trim the hedges, wash the dog, clean out the car, or do without anything!

The first few months of their marriage were tough ones for both Tad and Stefanie. More than once, Stefanie phoned her mother in tears as she faced five white shirts to iron and a husband who came home too tired to go out to eat. More than once, Tad drove around the block an extra time before he felt like coming home to a sad and angry bride. More than once, they argued about housekeeping and yard care. It took a mediator to help them sort out the chores of daily life.

Each must share with the other expectations of what to receive and what to give. Be very practical. If you don't intend to cook and clean, say so now. If you don't expect to mow the lawn, say so in advance. And if both of you do not expect to do the mundane chores that make for mutual living, who will do them, how will you earn the money to pay that person, and who will supervise that person's work?

What About Children?

If one of you doesn't want to have children, express that desire prior to marriage. Don't assume that you will talk your spouse into seeing things your way or that because he or she is silent on this point, both of you have the same goal.

How Many Children?

Be wary of the person who grew up as an only child and wants to have a dozen babies, or the future spouse who has in mind a definite number of children (and probably can tell you the sex of each, the order of birth, and the years apart they are in age). In discussing children, you will inevitably have to face two possibilities: (1) that you won't want all these children later, or (2) that you won't be able to give birth to these children.

For reasons that still somewhat baffle scientists, infertility is on the rise in our nation. We do know that married couples are waiting until older ages to have children, and those who follow this pattern are having fewer children. Expectations about numbers of children often change after marriage.

Perhaps the better questions to discuss in advance of marriage are these: What if we can't have children of our own? Is it possible that we won't want to have children? What will be our criteria to determine how many children we will have?

The subject of birth control is likely to arise in the wake of these questions. Ask yourselves, Will we use a form of birth control? If so, what method will we use?

Question your motives as individuals and as a couple for having children. What makes you want the size of family that you desire or keeps you from wanting children? Ask, Does either of us think that children will give us our identity or cause us to have greater value? Does either of us want children as a means of expressing personal power? Does either of us want children as a means of security?

Also question the ability of each to care for young children and to provide for them financially, physically, emotionally, and spiritually. Are both of you realistic as to the time and energy that children demand? Are you willing to delay many of your pleasures, desires, and commitments during the years you will be raising children to maturity?

Finally, keep in mind as you talk about your future roles as spouses and parents that you are talking about ideals and, to a great extent, dreams. A realistic expectation is that neither you nor your spouse will be able to live up to 100 percent of the goals you voice and certainly not 100 percent of the time.

COMPATIBILITY OF GOALS AND DREAMS

Work and Careers

Do you expect to have a career? A career is more than a job. A career nearly always denotes a consistent line of work that leads to increasingly higher levels of achievement and, with achievement, greater recognition and reward. People tend to hold jobs and chart careers.

Patterns of work affect compatibility in several ways. Ask yourselves, Do both of us expect to work outside the home? Is there a time when we anticipate that one of us will not be working? Is one or both of us committed to forging a career as opposed to just having a job? To what extent is work a part of each of our identities as individuals?

Do you regard yourself, for example, as an attorney, a doctor, a teacher, an executive, a nurse, an executive secretary, a shop manager, a foreman, a supervisor? If your career identity is significant to you, chances are, you will feel a void in your life if that job ends.

Memberships and Associations

What memberships and associations are important to each of you? Do you and your beloved share these interests? Talk about which memberships and affiliations you intend to maintain after you are married.

Nancy and Nick were into theater arts prior to their marriage. They met while they were trying out for a play. Nick often acted, directed, or worked as part of the crew for their community theater. Nancy was an actress, and when she wasn't on stage, she helped with promotion and ticket sales.

ARE WE COMPATIBLE?

They frequently attended productions in which they weren't involved directly. Both had full-time jobs in the health-care profession.

After the birth of their daughter, Nancy and Nick faced an important decision: Who is going to stay with the baby at night? Theater rehearsals usually follow an intense schedule that can last a period of several weeks. Nancy opted to stay home, and Nick continued to be active in the theater. Over time, Nancy began to resent the fun Nick continued to have with their theater buddies. Nick offered to stay home with the baby so that Nancy could be involved, but she felt guilty leaving their child. And she didn't really trust Nick's parenting skills.

Years went by and Nancy and Nick faced a widening gap in their marriage. They had very little that they could call a mutual life, apart from sleeping in the same house for a few hours each night. They worked in different locations across town from each other and kept different schedules. Nancy was up to her ears in PTA activities and her daughter's school plays, while Nick continued to be involved in community theater.

In facing the lack of mutuality in their lives, Nick was unwilling to give up some of his theater time; Nancy didn't feel she could compromise her involvement with their child. The two eventually separated and live in separate homes, although they are still legally married.

Finding a mutuality of nonwork interests is important in a relationship. Two partners in a marriage should have activities that they can share and that are enjoyable or fulfilling to each person.

COMPATIBILITY OF GOALS AND DREAMS

Ask yourselves, What do we envision doing as a couple apart from work and outside the home? What do we plan to attend? To what do we plan to belong?

Anticipating Change

There's no way for you or your intended spouse to predict the changes you may encounter as the months and years of your marriage unfold. You cannot predict the level of success you might achieve. You cannot anticipate fully the trials or triumphs you might encounter.

But you can appraise prior to marriage your compatibility in these ways: How have you responded in the past when a dream was deferred? How has your beloved one responded? What goals in the past has each reached as the result of planning and hard work? Are there goals that you set but didn't achieve? Why not? How have you dealt with failures? What has been the pattern of memberships in the past? Have you been loyal, long-standing members, or have you been sporadic, short-term members?

Dreams Deferred

Work toward seeing goals reached and dreams realized is often delayed by life's circumstances. Ask yourselves, How do I and my beloved respond when we hit the snags or detours that impede our progress toward reaching our goals? Do we blame ourselves without mercy? Do we blame others? Do we blame each other? Do we continue to move forward, perhaps pacing ourselves differently or adjusting our expectations?

Look for these critical traits in yourself and your beloved:

ARE WE COMPATIBLE?

○ Patience. Are you willing to persevere over time? Are you willing to let others catch up to you when it comes to group goals, including family goals?

○ Persistence. Do you continue to pursue your goal, or do you give up? Do you continue to work toward your goal with concerted effort and firm belief?

○ Responsibility. Do you take your share of responsibility for any failures or setbacks that you experience along the way toward reaching a goal?

Mardell helped his girlfriend, Solana, baby-sit one evening. He said, "I saw how patient she was with each child and with my lack of childcare skills. I fell in love with her that very evening!"

Len asked out Kitty five times before she finally said yes. She saw in him one of his main traits as a person: persistence.

Boyd watched Billie go through the rise and fall of her catering company. He watched her regain her optimism for living, pay off her debts, and pursue a new venture—this time, to success. He said, "It didn't matter to me that Billie failed in the gourmet business. What mattered was what she did after she failed. I saw in her determination. She took responsibility. I wanted those traits in a wife. The way I look at it, Billie has what it takes to endure hard times and keep fighting. Now, I'm not eager for hard times, but life in itself is hard. I feel as if I can trust Billie to fight the battles with me and not sit down and quit."

Patience, diligence, and responsibility are traits of a mature, psychologically healthy person.

COMPATIBILITY OF GOALS AND DREAMS

Dreams Dashed

At times, dreams hit a dead end. The end of the line might be the loss of a job, the final event of a career, or the death of a loved one. Sometimes a goal moves from being achievable to being unachievable. That's a hard reality for some to face.

Ask yourself, Have there been times in the past when my beloved was forced to call it quits? Did he or she do so graciously? Did he fight the reality of the situation? Was she able to look forward to a new chapter in her life with optimism?

How we face failure is a real test of character at any time, but especially so, it seems, within a marriage. We don't want to disappoint the one we love.

A normal period of mourning for any loss of a goal is understandable. The significant aspect of failure, though, is the ability to rebound within a reasonable length of time and to deal with the loss in a healthy way.

Ask your beloved, "How did you feel in the wake of that failure? What did you decide to do? What was most helpful to you during that period?" If your beloved answers that he felt nothing, that he didn't make a decision (but went with the flow of the times), and that nothing anybody did or said was of any help, be concerned.

Also be wary if your beloved reports no failures in her life. She is being very unrealistic, she is being dishonest, or she truly has led a charmed life and her experience with failure lies ahead. Every life is marked by failure at some point. My advice would be to wait until your beloved experiences a failure and see how she responds to it. Those who don't experience failures until fairly late in life tend to take failures very hard.

In facing a dream denied, both realism and optimism are traits to be desired.

Facing the Fear Factor

Are any of your goals or dreams rooted in fear? Are you motivated by what might not be or by threat?

Some people struggle for wealth because they are scared of poverty. Some people seek vast power because they once felt extremely weak. Other people desire fame because they had low self-esteem in earlier years. Still others are motivated to succeed because they fear failure.

Ask yourselves as you discuss marriage, Is either of us motivated toward goals and dreams out of fear? If so, what are those fears?

Bob was afraid of failing his demanding father, whom he worshiped secretly but criticized openly. To earn his father's blessing, he married a young woman he thought his father would like. He insisted that she do, say, and behave in ways that his father would judge as good. He demanded perfection from his wife because he wanted to present perfection to his father. He was extremely afraid of losing his father's approval. In the process, he lost his wife. No woman could live up to the perfection Bob required.

Unchecked fear results in unhealthy behavior. It greatly impedes progress toward reaching goals and dreams. If you suspect that your beloved is motivated by fear, don't marry unless that fear is unmasked, and healing can begin to take place.

COMPATIBILITY OF GOALS AND DREAMS

A Quiz to Identify Compatibility of Goals and Dreams

The "Compatibility of Goals and Dreams Quiz" is aimed at identifying the areas in which you and your beloved are compatible. The top set of continuums is related to objective issues that you should have given some thought to before marriage. The bottom set of continuums relates to your ability to achieve goals and overcome failures.

In most cases, people are pretty good at looking at their own track records and observing their goal-related traits. These continuums are headlined simply by an "I" statement.

Take your life as a whole in marking these continuums. Go with your first instinctual response. Push your responses to the outer edges rather than choose to occupy a safe middle position on the continuum.

I...

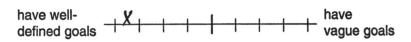

have well-defined goals ———————————————— have vague goals

In looking at her life, the person who marked the continuum above felt that she had well-defined personal goals but vague professional goals. Her personal goals, however, were the ones she valued the most and put the most effort into, so she edged her response toward the well-defined side of the continuum.

After you have marked the bottom set of continuums, take a second look at each item with this question in mind: What evidence is there to support my claim? If you don't feel you

COMPATIBILITY OF GOALS
AND DREAMS QUIZ

PERSON A

Mark your opinions and desires on the form below, exaggerating your responses slightly toward the outer edges of the continuum.

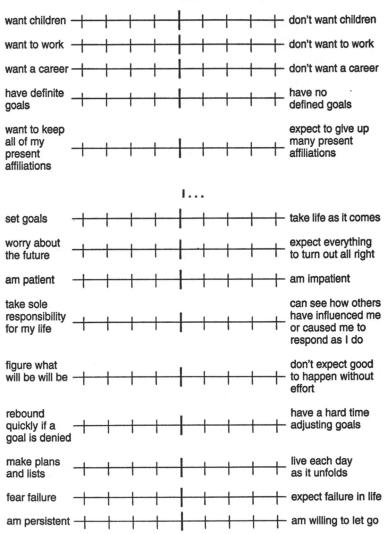

I...

want children ┤├─┼─┼─┼─┼─┼─┼─┼─┼─├ don't want children

want to work ┤├─┼─┼─┼─┼─┼─┼─┼─┼─├ don't want to work

want a career ┤├─┼─┼─┼─┼─┼─┼─┼─┼─├ don't want a career

have definite goals ┤├─┼─┼─┼─┼─┼─┼─┼─┼─├ have no defined goals

want to keep all of my present affiliations ┤├─┼─┼─┼─┼─┼─┼─┼─┼─├ expect to give up many present affiliations

I...

set goals ┤├─┼─┼─┼─┼─┼─┼─┼─┼─├ take life as it comes

worry about the future ┤├─┼─┼─┼─┼─┼─┼─┼─┼─├ expect everything to turn out all right

am patient ┤├─┼─┼─┼─┼─┼─┼─┼─┼─├ am impatient

take sole responsibility for my life ┤├─┼─┼─┼─┼─┼─┼─┼─┼─├ can see how others have influenced me or caused me to respond as I do

figure what will be will be ┤├─┼─┼─┼─┼─┼─┼─┼─┼─├ don't expect good to happen without effort

rebound quickly if a goal is denied ┤├─┼─┼─┼─┼─┼─┼─┼─┼─├ have a hard time adjusting goals

make plans and lists ┤├─┼─┼─┼─┼─┼─┼─┼─┼─├ live each day as it unfolds

fear failure ┤├─┼─┼─┼─┼─┼─┼─┼─┼─├ expect failure in life

am persistent ┤├─┼─┼─┼─┼─┼─┼─┼─┼─├ am willing to let go

COMPATIBILITY OF GOALS
AND DREAMS QUIZ

PERSON B

Mark your opinions and desires on the form below, exaggerating your responses slightly toward the outer edges of the continuum.

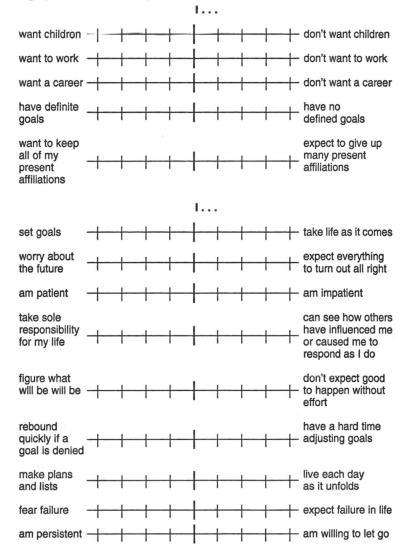

want children	don't want children
want to work	don't want to work
want a career	don't want a career
have definite goals	have no defined goals
want to keep all of my present affiliations	expect to give up many present affiliations
set goals	take life as it comes
worry about the future	expect everything to turn out all right
am patient	am impatient
take sole responsibility for my life	can see how others have influenced me or caused me to respond as I do
figure what will be will be	don't expect good to happen without effort
rebound quickly if a goal is denied	have a hard time adjusting goals
make plans and lists	live each day as it unfolds
fear failure	expect failure in life
am persistent	am willing to let go

could justify the mark you have given yourself with some form of evidence, rethink and remark the form.

Evaluating Your Responses

Transfer your responses to the form "Your Compatibility of Goals and Dreams as a Couple."

Again, connect the marks with vertical lines. Identify areas in which you and your beloved are naturally compatible. Note areas of incompatibility.

In marking some of your goal-related abilities and traits, you are revealing your perception of yourself to your future partner. If your intended spouse challenges your perception, hear him or her out. Make sure that he or she bolsters the arguments with examples or evidence. Weigh the comments seriously.

If you believe strongly in the accuracy of your mark, however, don't be dissuaded. You may not have revealed certain characteristics to your beloved. Recognize that he or she holds an opinion of you that may not be accurate, and seek to correct that perception over time, not through argument.

The longer the two of you date or are engaged, the greater the likelihood that your goals, dreams, and desires regarding marriage, children, careers, and associations may change. If you change your mind about a significant matter, such as no longer desiring to have children with your intended spouse or no longer desiring to pursue a career, discuss that change openly and fully. Be prepared to give a cause for the change.

In order for a marriage to endure and be satisfying, the partners must find a level of consistency. One person, or both, cannot be continually in flux regarding goals and

YOUR COMPATIBILITY
OF GOALS AND DREAMS
AS A COUPLE

Transfer your marks to the form below. It does not matter which marks belong to which person. Connect the marks to create two vertical lines. The gap between the two sets of marks reflects your compatibility of goals and dreams as a couple.

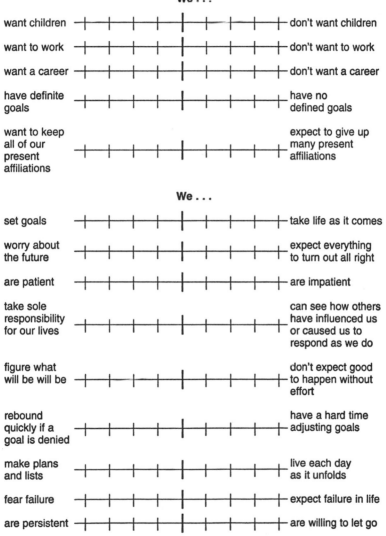

We . . .

want children	don't want children
want to work	don't want to work
want a career	don't want a career
have definite goals	have no defined goals
want to keep all of our present affiliations	expect to give up many present affiliations

We . . .

set goals	take life as it comes
worry about the future	expect everything to turn out all right
are patient	are impatient
take sole responsibility for our lives	can see how others have influenced us or caused us to respond as we do
figure what will be will be	don't expect good to happen without effort
rebound quickly if a goal is denied	have a hard time adjusting goals
make plans and lists	live each day as it unfolds
fear failure	expect failure in life
are persistent	are willing to let go

ARE WE COMPATIBLE?

dreams. Be wary if your beloved wants one thing one day and something quite different the next, only to change his or her mind a week later.

Ask, Has my beloved been committed to the same goals for a sufficient amount of time to test whether the goals are achievable and make some progress toward reaching them?

As your marriage progresses, you may desire to reach new goals or pursue new dreams that neither person anticipated prior to marriage. That tends to happen when a person reaches previously set goals. Enjoy the process of setting new goals together!

Chapter 8

COMPATIBILITY OF VALUES

To a great extent, personality traits appear to be defined at birth. Parents are often amazed at the traits they see in their infants. These personality traits are subject to the will in terms of their expression and are therefore subject to training, but they are pretty much a part of us from birth.

The "Stuff" of Our Inner Nature

Our values, on the other hand, are learned. They are the guides that are implanted in us from our earliest memories. Our values substantially shape the way we express our personalities. They provide boundaries for what we know as good and bad. They are the principles by which we live. They are the standards by which we gauge our success and ascribe meaning to life experiences.

ARE WE COMPATIBLE?

Since parents are our primary teachers, we learn most of our values from them. If we are part of an extended family, community, and church body that reinforce the values we have learned in the home, our values tend to become quite ingrained by the time we reach puberty. If we have no mediating experiences, by the time we reach adulthood, our values are set to the point that they are nearly impossible to change.

Behavior is subject to change, of course. We can learn new ways to express our values and personalities. But in the main, the core values of our lives are fairly well established by the time we are ready for marriage.

Values are the "stuff" of our inner nature. They are the true essence of who we are, and they are at the root of our ability to learn, grow, change, and adapt—all of which must happen for a marriage to last.

How Much Change Is Possible?

As you prepare for marriage, keep in mind that you will not be able to change your intended spouse very much, if at all. At the very best, you can hope for some adjustment of behaviors so that the two of you can live together peaceably.

But don't go into marriage expecting any type of major overhaul or reform in your beloved as the result of marriage itself or your influence as a spouse. It simply doesn't happen.

Elizabeth came to talk to me one day. "I thought my love would give Eric the security he needed," she said with a giant sigh.

"Security?" I asked.

"Eric grew up without a stable home life," she explained.

COMPATIBILITY OF VALUES

"Before Eric was ten years old, he had moved nine times and had gone to six different schools in three states."

"What were the specific changes you were hoping to see in Eric?" I asked.

"I thought he'd relax a little and calm down as a person. I thought he'd want to settle down and have a stable home."

"And?" I asked.

"He's been employed by his company for only a year, and we've lived in our current apartment only six months. He's already talking about changing jobs and moving to another city. If anything, he seems more wound up than he was before we married."

Elizabeth hadn't realized that Eric was born energetic and ready to conquer the world. The values he had acquired as a child did not stress a stable environment; the values placed importance on a person's ability to cope with changes and find inner stability despite external fluctuation.

Eric didn't fear change; his inner stability allowed him to stay centered, no matter the environment. Elizabeth was the one who struggled with stability! Her family values stressed maintenance of the status quo. Her personality resisted change of any type.

The likelihood that Elizabeth might change Eric? Slim to none.

Over the next three years, Eric received two promotions, and he and Elizabeth made two moves. Eric remained in high gear in personality and in his career. When he was offered a third promotion that entailed yet another move, he opted to commute to the new job. He said, "I'll probably be moved within the company again in a year or so, and who knows where that will be? It's important now for Elizabeth to have a few years in the same house."

For her part, Elizabeth came to appreciate Eric's successes and to see that his high energy had first attracted her to him. She admitted, "If Eric slowed down, he wouldn't be Eric."

Core Values to Seek Out

What then are the values that a person should seek out when evaluating a potential mate? What makes for good husband material or good wife material?

Six values must be held in common for a marriage to endure and be satisfying to both persons. These values are at the core of any long-term relationship, especially a marriage: (1) truthfulness, (2) selflessness, (3) realistic optimism, (4) empathy, (5) work ethic, and (6) willingness to communicate. We'll take a look at each in turn.

Value Number 1: Truthfulness

No one has a corner on the truth. The Scriptures tell us that truth is as the grains of sand on the sea. Each person sees absolute truth from a finite and unique perspective. Our collective understanding of truth is far more valuable than our individual understanding of it.

We can, however, speak truth openly, as best we know it. We can be honest with each other in expressing our opinions and ideas. We can offer information when we believe it will be helpful to another person.

As an interesting exercise in preparation for marriage, each person makes a list of at least five statements (and no more than ten) that each believes to be true. Then they compare lists and talk about these truths. One conclusion that is nearly always drawn in such an exercise is that we nearly always have evidence for the truths we hold, and that evidence nearly always involves other people.

We may believe this statement: "Love conquers all." How do we know that to be true? We can't fully know the truth of that statement unless we have had a personal experience in which love did conquer an unwanted emotion.

Another conclusion that we draw about truth is that it is very personal. Each person has a different perspective on absolute truth, and each person knows truth at a very deep, intuitive level. Sometimes we don't know why we believe certain things; we just do.

In expressing truth, keep in mind that the truth you speak is from your perspective and based on your experience. When you open yourself up to hearing the truth of others— from their perspective and based on their experience—you need to expect that at least some of what you have held to be true isn't! Expect to have your thinking changed a little.

Be wary of the person who claims to know all there is to know—and to know it with complete assurance. Be wary of the person who says, "*This* is the way it is." A far easier person to live with prefaces opinions and ideas with statements such as, "This is how I see things . . . ," or "In my experience . . . ," or "From my point of view. . . ."

Ask as you and your beloved prepare for marriage, Are we open to hearing the opinions and ideas of others? Does either of us claim to have a corner on the truth?

ARE WE COMPATIBLE?

Recognizing a Lie

Part of knowing the truth is recognizing or acknowledging lies. Most of us are probably better at discerning lies than we are in defining truth.

Lies always diminish or destroy. They separate people, cause harm, and inhibit. Lies are rooted in power, intimidation, and manipulation. They kill relationships.

The truth builds up and creates. It binds people together, heals, and causes people to expand their horizons. Truth is rooted in love. It enriches relationships.

Nearly all of us buy into lies or misrepresentations at one time or other in our lives—consciously or unconsciously. We are all guilty of telling lies, inadvertently or purposefully. The ability to recognize deception is valuable.

Ask yourselves, Are we open to hearing the truth from each other, or do we prefer to accept lies at face value?

Speaking Honestly

Knowing truth and speaking truthfully—or honestly—are two different things. Honesty is speaking openly and candidly the things that you believe to be truth or that you perceive to be lies. Advice given honestly can and should be couched in terms that cause it to be more acceptable to the hearer.

Ask yourselves, Are we open to hearing honest statements from each other? Do we give and receive the statements readily and with a spirit of love?

Note how your beloved speaks to friends. Is he honest in his communication with them? Does she confront lies?

Compatibility of Values

Is your beloved candid with you when it comes to telling you that you are getting on his or her nerves, that your slip is showing, that your tie is crooked, or that your latest joke is inappropriate? Honesty must extend into all areas of communication and be pervasive in both speech and behavior.

Value Number 2: Selflessness

Marriage requires selfless behaviors. As one person put it, "Self is sacrificed on the altar of US." To a great extent, that is true.

For a relationship to be healthy, each person must maintain a strong individual identity. Each must be true to the unique personality and attributes and succeed in abilities and capabilities. Each person must also be willing to deny some desires for the sake of the beloved and the sake of the union.

Ask yourself, Does my beloved always insist on having his or her way? Do I insist on having my way all of the time?

You should be able to point to some concrete examples in your dating or engagement relationship in which your beloved yielded to your desires and you yielded to your beloved's desires.

No one is required to be the doormat on which another person wipes his or her feet. At the same time, you are to be extremely flexible in giving of your material substance, time, energy, skill, and wisdom to others, and in deferring your will to that of others in order to maintain the peace.

No one person in a marriage should do all the giving or all the receiving.

Value Number 3: Realistic Optimism

Optimism is the ability to feel hopeful about the future, even if present circumstances are devastating. Realistic optimism is tempered by a realistic expectation that the future will be better than the present, even though time, effort, and change may be involved.

We often refer to very optimistic people as being eternal optimists. They are always expecting to see a rainbow emerge from the dark clouds and to find a pot of gold at the end of it. Unfortunately, eternal optimists often spend more of their time expecting than doing. They don't make the connection between work and reward; their focus is solely on the glorious end result.

Realistic optimists look for better days and are willing to work, adjust, and persevere in making better days happen.

Be wary of marrying an eternal optimist.

Realistic optimists, on the other hand, are a joy to live with and work alongside. No matter what the situation or circumstance—including a problem or an incompatibility gap in a marriage—they are willing to work to resolve the problem or bridge the gap in anticipation of a better tomorrow.

Note what your beloved says about the future. Does he or she hold out hope for a world that is very bright? Don't squelch that dream. Do look, however, for evidence that he or she is willing to work to make that dream happen.

Does your optimistic beloved one believe the bright new world is going to happen suddenly or overnight? Does he or she think it will happen as a matter of luck, good fortune, or windfall? What plans is he or she making to enhance the coming of that day or that circumstance?

COMPATIBILITY OF VALUES

Realism is not the opposite of optimism, which is what eternal optimists sometimes think. The opposite of optimism is pessimism—a dastardly trait. The pessimist rarely wants to work on marriage problems or bridge incompatibility gaps. Rather, the pessimist sees divorce as an inevitable conclusion. Recognize, though, that pessimism can come in spurts. Expect your future spouse to have moments of discouragement, even periods of lethargy or mild depression. That's life. But beware of marrying the person who seems perpetually to be under a dark cloud.

Value Number 4: Empathy

Empathy is the ability to feel what another person is feeling—truly to walk in the other's shoes emotionally, psychologically, or spiritually. The empathic person is sensitive to another person's need and deeply desires to help.

Ask about your beloved, To what extent can my beloved identify with people who are suffering? Does he or she reach out to people in need and help them?

Take note of the ways in which your beloved shows concern for needy people. Does he want to fix all of their problems for them? Or does she get into the circumstance and work alongside the person in need until a solution is found? The latter is the empathic approach.

Be aware of these three tendencies in empathy:

1. A person tends to be more empathic if he or she has been through a similar circumstance or faced a similar situation.

2. A person tends to be more empathic toward others if he or she is not presently under great stress.
3. A person tends to be more empathic if he or she senses real danger, pain, or threat to another person.

The implications related to compatibility are parallel:

1. Don't expect your beloved to sense a hurt you are feeling if it lies in an area where you do not have natural harmony.
2. Don't expect your beloved to be sensitive to your pain if he or she is under great stress.
3. Don't expect your beloved to read your mind if the hurt you are feeling is primarily emotional, spiritual, or psychological.

Empathy versus Sympathy

Empathy and sympathy are not the same. Sympathy is feeling sorrow for another person's pain or need. Pity is feeling sympathy without hope that the situation can change. Empathy is identifying with the pain while attempting to alleviate it. Empathy has active and hopeful components.

In a marriage, an empathic person is not going to sit on the sidelines of problems you encounter as a couple (either in your relationship or in life) and wring her hands, bemoan the situation, and feel sorry for herself or for you. She is going to be moved by the problem to the point of action. He is going to confront what is wrong and attempt to right it. He is going to work for a solution within the relationship rather than flee it.

COMPATIBILITY OF VALUES

Value Number 5: Work Ethic

Earlier, we discussed work and focused on employment and earning power. Here, we are focusing on work as effort and expenditure of energy. The degree to which you value work, or effort, affects not only your physical and material lives but all aspects of a relationship.

People with a strong work ethic work and place high value on work. They see work as an integral part of living. People with a weak work ethic may work but tend to do so grudgingly. They tend to see work as something they do so that they can pay for a life that begins when the work ends.

Ask about your beloved, Is my beloved just as enthusiastic about a workday morning as a nonworkday morning? Does my beloved live for weekends and vacations, or is work an important and integral part of life? How does my beloved value chores related to our home or the achievement of our family goals?

People with a healthy work ethic are not necessarily workaholics, those who work two jobs, or those who try to accumulate forty hours of overtime each pay period. Rather, people with a healthy work ethic tend to work hard and then appreciate rest and relish in reward.

People with a healthy work ethic know that anything of value in life requires effort. They don't expect a good marriage to be automatic or immediate.

A healthy work ethic is a highly prized trait in a marriage partner, especially in those areas of incompatibility in which you need to forge an agreement. The person who values work is likely to be far more willing to put effort into bridging differences.

ARE WE COMPATIBLE?

Ask about your beloved, Does he or she live to work or work to live? Does he put his best effort into everything he does? Does she resent the fact that she has to work or exert effort to make something happen?

Be wary of the person who expects others to work on his behalf, or who is always willing to let others pay. Also be wary of the person who expects God to provide to the point that he or she has to do nothing. James taught, "Faith by itself, if it does not have works, is dead" (James 2:17). Paul taught, "If anyone will not work, neither shall he eat" (2 Thess. 3:10). The person who expects God to provide without any effort on his or her part is grounded not in faith but in presumption.

The Value of Discipline

The work ethic is closely linked to discipline. Disciplined people pace themselves to accommodate both work and rest. They value both giving and receiving. They understand that life has consequences.

People with a healthy work ethic are likely to be disciplined physically, materially, and spiritually. They are likely to practice what they preach and "walk their talk." They are likely to value self-discipline in others. People with a strong work ethic tend to be self-starters, highly motivated to accomplish the work they see to do.

Within marriage, self-starters will not wait for compatibility to click into place but will seek out ways to enhance compatibility and keep agreements strong. They are likely to need, desire, and work hard to maintain the consistency of a relationship. They are far more likely to be loyal and faithful.

COMPATIBILITY OF VALUES

Ask of your beloved, Is he or she disciplined, or does my beloved wait for others to dictate what should be done or not done? Is my beloved self-motivated, quick to jump into action, or does he or she wait to be prodded?

The stronger your work ethic, the more important it is that you marry a person with a strong work ethic. If you have a strong work ethic and you marry someone who has a weak one, you are likely to be frustrated at what you perceive to be laziness, lack of discipline, and lack of ambition.

Value Number 6: Willingness to Communicate

You don't need to be an excellent communicator to be a good spouse. The communication in marriage does not need to be frequent or intense. But for a marriage to be mutually satisfying and enduring, both partners must be willing to communicate with each other. Both must value communication to the point that they are willing to leap the hurdles of their insecurities, weaknesses, and shyness and reach out in words and meaningful deeds to each other.

Every person is capable of communicating (at some level, to some degree). The ability to communicate is part of human life. A lack of communication in marriage is never a matter of "we can't communicate." The problem is always a matter of "one of us, at least, doesn't *want* to communicate."

Ask yourself, Are there ever times when my beloved totally withdraws and refuses to communicate? Are there times when I feel that my beloved is using silence to punish me or to convey a message that I don't understand? Be concerned if your answer is yes to either question. If this behavior exists during the golden glow of courtship days, it is only likely to increase after marriage vows are said.

Respect differences in communication style. Shyness and privacy are different from a willful use of silence, a refusal to communicate even though one is capable of it and generally has a message to convey. Be wary of the person who uses silence as a means of punishing, manipulating, or exerting control.

The only way to bridge differences and find agreement in areas where natural compatibility does not exist is by means of communication. Both partners must be willing to reveal, as candidly as possible, how they feel, what they want, and who they are.

In sum, the person who doesn't value communication to the point of being willing to communicate is a person who doesn't truly value relationship. And that is a person who is not capable of valuing marriage.

Valuing Marriage

When all of the compatibility quizzes have been taken and analyzed, perhaps the two most important questions that remain are these: Do both of you really want to be married? Do both of you really want to be married to each other?

More than two decades ago, I had a skilled and wise college professor who taught communication arts. Prior to his work in academia, he and his wife had pastored several churches. I was one of several students invited to their home one evening for conversation and coffee. The topic of marriage came up.

COMPATIBILITY OF VALUES

We all voiced our opinions about what made for a good marriage. He and his wife listened thoughtfully. One of us finally asked, "What do you think, Doctor?"

He said, "In all our years of pastoring and counseling couples, we have seen the most unlikely pairs. We've spent thousands of hours, literally, in marriage counseling during the last three decades, and there's only one thing we've found that truly makes for a lasting marriage."

"What is that?" one of the students asked eagerly.

"Both people must want to be married to each other more than they want to divorce."

I've witnessed the wisdom of his reply again and again in my conversations and counseling sessions related to marriage.

In the end, couples stay together because they want to stay together. Their marriages endure not so much as a matter of love as a matter of committed will.

Keeping Commitments

Take a look at the ability of your beloved to make and keep commitments in the past. Is he a person of his word? Does she do what she says she is going to do? Can he stick with something, regardless of adversity? That will tell you something of your beloved's ability to keep a commitment.

Discovering Opinions About Marriage

Note how your beloved speaks about marriage. Does she refer to it as a ball and chain, a prison, an institution, the end of life, a trap? Even when spoken in jest, these comments can reveal how a person feels about marriage—that it is confining and misery-laden.

ARE WE COMPATIBLE?

How does your beloved feel about his parents' marriage? If the impression is negative, what makes you believe that your beloved will have a different impression about your relationship?

Compatibility is never 100 percent. No surgery makes you "one." No emotional rewiring or intellectual bonding makes you inseparable. People enter into marriage *willfully*, regardless of prevailing circumstances, pressures, or passion. They forge agreements in areas of incompatibility *willfully*. They stay together *willfully*.

Ask your beloved directly, "How do you envision your life ten years from now? Twenty years from now?"

Listen closely. Does she envision herself being married to you? If not, be concerned! If so, ask, "Do you think you will be happily married?" If not, find out why. If the answer is yes, ask, "What makes you think so?"

Finally, ask your beloved, "Do you think that I will be happily married ten years from now? Why?"

You can never fully anticipate the propensity of your beloved to stay married or to fulfill his vow to love you until death parts you. But you can hear how your beloved speaks of marriage and the value she places at the present time on having a long and enduring marriage.

A person who desires to be married, now and all of life, is likely to work at fulfilling that desire.

The Compatibility of Values Quiz

On the following pages, you will find the "Compatibility of Values Quiz." Each person is asked to make a mark on a series of continuums between two values, which are not necessarily true opposites.

Your response to these value-laden words and phrases is likely to be mostly intuitive. Go with your first impulse. Select which word or phrase is more comfortable to you. Again, exaggerate your position slightly toward the word or phrase you favor. The closer you are to an outer edge, the stronger your response.

Mark your forms now.

COMPATIBILITY OF
VALUES QUIZ

PERSON A

Place an X closest to the word or phrase with the greatest meaning or the greatest value for you. Exaggerate your position slightly toward the outer edge of the continuum.

Value Positions

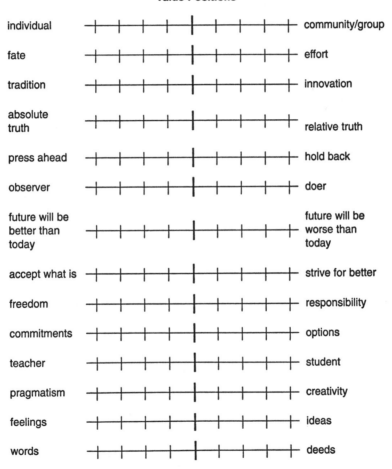

individual   community/group

fate   effort

tradition   innovation

absolute truth   relative truth

press ahead   hold back

observer   doer

future will be better than today   future will be worse than today

accept what is   strive for better

freedom   responsibility

commitments   options

teacher   student

pragmatism   creativity

feelings   ideas

words   deeds

COMPATIBILITY OF
VALUES QUIZ

PERSON B

Place an X closest to the word or phrase with the greatest meaning or the greatest value for you. Exaggerate your position slightly toward the outer edge of the continuum.

Value Positions

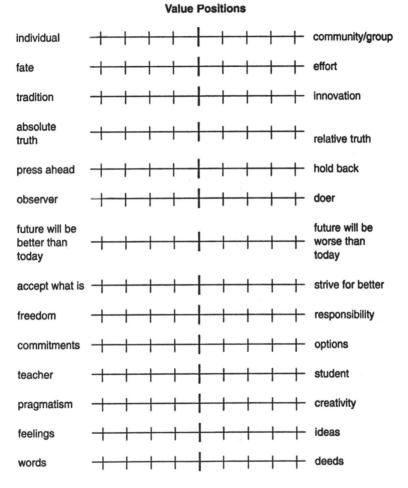

individual	community/group
fate	effort
tradition	innovation
absolute truth	relative truth
press ahead	hold back
observer	doer
future will be better than today	future will be worse than today
accept what is	strive for better
freedom	responsibility
commitments	options
teacher	student
pragmatism	creativity
feelings	ideas
words	deeds

ARE WE COMPATIBLE?

Evaluating Your Responses

On the "Values Compatibility" form, compile your answers to the "Compatibility of Values Quiz." As on previous compilation forms, you do not need to note which mark belongs to which person. After you have marked all of your responses, draw a vertical line connecting the opposing positions.

Look closely at the widest gaps. These are the areas about which to be most concerned. The gaps reflect a significant discrepancy in the importance you have placed on certain values key to a good marriage.

Talk about why you gave strong marks to certain value positions. Also talk about any value statements that you believe to be irrelevant to marriage or unimportant in general.

Your discussion of these values may very well be one of the most important discussions you have prior to your marriage, and certainly one that is likely to give both of you a great sense of encouragement or food for thought.

On this quiz, you have expressed what you believe, not necessarily what you *do*. Talk about that with your beloved. Is there a value here with which you agree but fail to comply? Are you courageous enough to admit it?

When you are alone, reflect on the entire scope of your relationship with your beloved. Are there discrepancies between what he or she has said about values and the way in which he or she has acted toward you or in your presence?

Be wary if your beloved refuses to admit to any discrepancies between what he holds in high regard and how he lives his life. No one is capable of perfectly living out what she says she believes.

VALUES COMPATIBILITY

Transfer your responses to the form below. You do not need to be concerned about which mark belongs to which person. Connect your marks in a vertical fashion to form two lines.

Our Value Positions

individual	community/group
fate	effort
tradition	innovation
absolute truth	relative truth
press ahead	hold back
observer	doer
future will be better than today	future will be worse than today
accept what is	strive for better
freedom	responsibility
commitments	options
teacher	student
pragmatism	creativity
feelings	ideas
words	deeds

Finally, reflect on your discussion about these value-laden words and phrases. Were both of you comfortable discussing these value statements? Was there a genuine give-and-take in your conversation? Did one person claim to have the right priorities and see the other person's responses as in error? Was one of you adamant about any value to the exclusion of other values?

The person who has only one or two strongly held values about which he is primarily concerned may be on a soapbox about those values or see all of life through their filter. Such a person is likely to be fairly narrow-minded and see little room for compromise with people who hold other opinions.

Conversely, the person who holds no strongly held values is likely to be fairly wishy-washy and unpredictable.

Value differences are among the most difficult gaps to bridge in a relationship because they are so deeply ingrained. If you don't like what you see now, or don't believe you can live with some of the most strongly held values your beloved expresses, you may be better off ending your relationship.

When two people hold similar values, they have a strong base on which to bridge gaps in other areas of their lives. Be encouraged if this is your situation as a couple!

Chapter 9

Forging Agreement in Areas of Difference

As you and your beloved have taken the various compatibility-oriented quizzes in this book, you no doubt have isolated several areas of incompatibility.

If you and your beloved do not register *any* incompatibility, one or both are probably in denial or in fear. No two people are identical or completely compatible in all areas of their lives.

As you and your beloved attempt to bridge areas of incompatibility, think of yourselves not as negotiators but as teammates. The appropriate stance to take is not one of opposite sides but one of being on the same larger side. Each person has a unique position, to be sure, but each person must also keep in mind the greater whole of the relationship.

Finding agreement is not a matter of one person's opinion holding sway over the other person's. Neither is it the outcome of a win-lose battle. Agreement is not mere compromise, although compromise may be involved. *Agreement is finding a solution that works equally well for both parties in the greater whole.*

To truly reach agreement, both persons considering the marriage must enter into bridge-building discussions from this perspective. Both must hold to the position, "We're in this together. We want this to work. Let's figure out what works best for us. Let's agree on a way to live."

Your Relationship Is Unique

All relationships have certain things in common, yet all are unique. No two people relate in precisely the same way.

Don't expect to find your agreements in a textbook, a couples guide, or the relationship enjoyed by another couple. You and your beloved need to find out what works for the two of you.

After marriage, some couples opt for separate bedrooms. Others wouldn't dream of sharing a bed larger than a standard double.

Some couples have widely divergent schedules and live in different cities. Others work in the same location and share two-room apartments.

Some couples come halfway around the world to find each other. Others grew up as next-door neighbors.

FORGING AGREEMENT

Some couples go different ways to church meetings, holiday celebrations, and vacation destinations. Others spend every day of every year together.

Some fight vigorously and then passionately make up. Others never seem to raise their voices at each other and are content with little physical intimacy.

In finding what works for you and your beloved, plan a way of living that works equally well for both of you. The goal is a win-win situation—a way of living that is enjoyable and satisfying for both spouses.

The Goal Is a Win-Win Situation

In facing the prospect of building bridges of agreement, you usually have two possibilities: (1) narrow the gap through mutual change, or (2) agree to accommodate differences.

Change to Narrow the Gap

The first decision you must make in building a bridge is whether it is possible to move closer together in your respective positions. This requires giving on both parts. Each person must change a little for compatibility gaps to narrow.

Change is sometimes tough. Sometimes a trial period is helpful to see if change is possible. As tough as change is to make, it is even tougher to maintain. Don't expect change to occur quickly or easily, or to be maintained without effort.

Remember that win-win situations are not built on one person winning and the other losing, or on one person changing and the other remaining the same. A win-win compromise requires change by both persons.

Accommodation

Another approach is to agree that the difference exists and to find ways of accommodating it.

Timing Is Everything

We've all heard the old saying, "Timing is everything." In confronting the differences you have with your beloved and in seeking to forge agreement, timing may not be everything, but it is extremely important.

The Timing for Change

Two aspects of timing warrant your attention. First is the timing that you allow yourselves for change and adaptation. Don't expect a marriage to be fully bonded the first month, the first year, or the first decade. In healthy marriages, couples continue to grow closer with each passing year.

Change is difficult, and so is accommodation. You have lived your life for probably twenty or more years before desiring to enter a committed relationship with your beloved. During that time, both of you have established certain routines and patterns of behavior. Changing those patterns of behavior won't happen overnight.

Sometimes a person is able to change a pattern of behavior fairly quickly only to experience a rebound effect later. Recognize that you and your beloved are probably going to be on your best behavior and trying your hardest the first few weeks or months of marriage, hence, the "honeymoon period." When a marriage truly settles in, many of your true incompatibilities may emerge, and the work of forming agreements begins.

Don't be disheartened. Hang in there. New habits take time to implement. You may need to work through several stages of adaptation before agreement occurs, and certainly before your relationship takes on an air of consistency.

Think in long-range terms, and give each other time to learn a new way of living.

The Timing of Confrontations

The second aspect of timing is this: choose carefully the times when you discuss your incompatibilities and attempt to bridge them.

Don't discuss change or adaptation you desire when one or both are

- feeling extreme stress at work or home.
- feeling intense anger, frustration, or any other emotion that is more intense than usual.
- under the influence of any chemical, including heavy-duty medications.
- physically exhausted.
- ill.
- reeling from a significant loss, such as the death of a loved one or loss of a job or business.

Give yourselves some time to cool off after an argument before you attempt to reconcile. Don't press for agreement.

Kendra grew up as an only child in a quiet, few-words-spoken home; voices were never raised. She could not recall a single incident in her childhood when one person had confronted another in displeasure. Her husband, Saul, grew up in a large intergenerational family characterized by lots of noise and confrontation. Voices were frequently raised in an effort to be heard above the din of sibling, parent, or grandparent voices. Dislikes were immediately labeled and confronted.

When Saul first confronted Kendra in the manner to which he was accustomed, Kendra felt that her marriage was on the brink of ending. Nobody had ever raised his voice at her, and she assumed that Saul was ready to leave her forever. She ran crying from the room, a response that confused Saul.

Saul ran after her, desiring to know what he had done to upset her. Of course, the tone and volume of his voice sounded more like a demand, and only heightened Kendra's fear and dismay. The louder Saul talked, the louder Kendra cried. The incident ended when Saul stormed out of the apartment.

When he returned, he was calmer and his voice softer. Kendra had time to think about what had happened. She told Saul how she had felt, and fortunately, he could see her point of view. Both obviously had some changing and adapting to do! They had several more conversations before Saul came to see fully that Kendra could not hear anything but the level of his voice when he shouted at her. Kendra became more bold in asking Saul to speak more softly. They now use this comment when they hear raised voices in their children: "Turn down the volume a little so I can hear you."

Here are specific suggestions as you and your beloved enter into a conversation about bridging incompatibilities:

Forging Agreement

1. Choose your issues and your timing carefully. Some issues are best confronted immediately. Others are best ignored until you see if a pattern is present or if an incident is isolated. Never wait to see if abusive behavior is repeated. As soon as the abuser has calmed down, confront the issue directly.

2. Don't press for too many changes at one time. Stay focused on a single issue. Don't bring up past disagreements or other areas of incompatibility. Don't generalize.

3. Never generalize about a person's personality.

4. Leave others out of the argument. Don't quote your parents or your friends. Don't compare yourselves to others. Don't invite friends in to choose sides.

5. Don't threaten the other person. Don't issue an ultimatum unless you fully intend to follow through on your statement.

For several years, Edna told Ned that she was going to divorce him. Sometimes the issues were great. Sometimes they were petty. Often they were related to things that Edna wanted to purchase for their home. Edna felt she had a suitable method for getting what she wanted from Ned since he always seemed to comply with her demands, at least temporarily. It was a technique she had watched her mother use for years.

Edna didn't realize that each time she threatened divorce, Ned thought she was serious. Over time, his self-esteem was severely eroded. If marriage to him was valued only at the price of a new set of kitchen curtains or a new bedspread, his "price" was pretty low. One day, Ned responded to Edna, "All right. Divorce me."

Edna, of course, didn't want a divorce. But Ned had reached his limit. He could no longer take the put-down of the threat.

Leave the word *divorce* out of your conversations with your spouse, especially conversations in which you are attempting to bridge an incompatibility gap. In fact, you might want to eliminate the word *divorce* from your vocabulary or your thinking.

In my experience with numerous frustrated, angry, and hurt couples, I have come to see that the more the word *divorce* is spoken between two people, or the more prominent it becomes in a person's thinking, the easier divorce begins to sound.

Divorce is rarely easy. It is nearly always painful and disruptive. It brings with it a great sense of loss—emotional, material, and/or spiritual.

Focus on the Solution

In discussing differences, do so only as a means of laying out on the table the various behaviors that you believe are in conflict. Don't let yourselves get bogged down at that point. Stay focused on reaching a solution.

Of the behaviors you've noted, which one is the most irritating or most troublesome to your finding a compatible way of living? Your solution should address that behavior.

Debby found it very difficult to express herself verbally in David's presence. In her words, "I'd get all tongue-tied. He's much more glib than I, and no matter what I would say, he'd find a way to twist my words so that I felt foolish."

FORGING AGREEMENT

Debby resorted to index cards. She'd write a succinct sentence on a card as to what she felt was a problem or area of incompatibility. On another card she'd write one possible solution that she thought she could live with. If there was more than one solution, she'd write each solution on a separate card.

When the time came that Debby felt she needed to confront David with the issue in question, she would give him the card with the problem stated on it and say, "I need to let you know that this is bothering me. I don't want to talk about it right now, but I would appreciate your taking this issue and writing down two or three win-win solutions that you think might work for us."

The cards gave David time to think through the problem and possible responses. He and Debby agreed that they could ask clarifying questions so that they fully understood the problem. David would then propose solutions. Debby would think about them. She'd offer her own solutions, and David would think about them. And once they finally sat down to talk, they were able to focus on solutions, rather than the initial problem.

Debby needed this much structure in dealing with their areas of incompatibility. David didn't, but he agreed to Debby's protocol.

They are the only couple I have ever met that used a card system for communicating, but the significant point is this: their method worked for them.

Another couple make appointments when they want to discuss an area of incompatibility. They meet in what they call their problem-solving cafe. They go there only when they are dealing with a problem. They sit on opposite sides of a booth and stay until they reach a tentative solution. They never go to the cafe for any other reason, and they refuse to bring confrontation into their condo or bring up issues at places they have come to enjoy fine dining.

Still another couple discuss incompatibilities only when they are driving together. The woman said, "That way, we don't have to look at each other. It's easier for both of us."

You may need to find an equally unusual way of signaling to your beloved that you perceive an incompatibility gap in your relationship and that you need to find a way of bridging it. You may need a very structured way of working out an agreement.

Timing and solution orientation are two vital factors in paving the way to successful agreement.

Consult a Third Party

In areas of personality difference or an incompatibility gap related to goals or values, couples sometimes cannot think of a win-win situation or stay cool, calm, and collected long enough for a rational discussion about their differences.

In those instances, a couple at odds may want to consult a third person. This third party may be a mutual friend or a trusted relative. Often, it is best to find a person who has a good reputation as a counselor but is entirely neutral in the relationship with both partners.

Professional psychologists and marriage therapists, licensed family counselors, and clergypersons are available for such consultations, as are a growing number of free counseling clinics staffed by persons trained to listen and offer suggestions. Older-and-wiser friends should not be overlooked.

Keep in mind as you go to a counselor that you are seeking a win-win solution, not a referee or someone who will take your side and reprimand your beloved.

What Higher Authority?

Who or what do you consider to be the highest authority over your life? What do you consider to be the ultimate source book for your life?

Do you and your beloved share this object of worship? Do you live by the same code and recognize the same book or creed as the bearer of ultimate truth? If so, you have common ground on which to build agreement.

Kori and Josh were at an impasse in their marriage. When they realized that they were squabbling with increasing frequency, that their marriage was becoming less satisfying to both of them, and that they were choosing to be apart as often as they were choosing to be together, they sought out the minister who married them. Both wanted to remain married. Both wanted to rekindle the love they had felt prior to their wedding and in the first few years of their marriage. They had isolated their differences but had sought no win-win agreement to bridge them. Rather, they had tended to ignore their differences in hopes that they would grow together naturally over time.

Their clergy counselor pointed out to them the importance of finding a way to live that was a win-win solution, and in a series of sessions, they explored various areas of incompatibility.

Kori and Josh found that the Bible had relevant things to say about each area of their incompatibility. "We got very good at looking things up in a concordance. We read aloud together everything that we could find in the Bible that related to marriage."

"And then," Kori added, "we went on to read everything we could find that related to friendship and then the parts that related to enemies and then the parts that described other relationships."

"Before we were through," Josh concluded, "we had read aloud nearly the entire Bible to each other. We found the Bible is a book about relationships and how to live in agreement with each other. Neither Kori nor I had a clue that the Bible held so many answers to questions and problems we faced."

One by one, Kori and Josh found ways to bridge their areas of incompatibility. Some solutions involved mutual change. Some solutions involved mutual acceptance of difference—agreeing to disagree. They developed new friends, new activities, and new ways of approaching problems. One of their shared activities was a Bible study class during which other young couples shared the solutions they were finding to problems in their marriages.

Ask yourselves as you anticipate marriage, Who is the higher authority to which we will turn in times of crisis? What is the authoritative set of guidelines by which we intend to live our lives?

FORGING AGREEMENT

Nothing Is Set in Concrete

Once you have come to a point of agreement—and have decided on changes, adaptations, or accommodations to implement—you need to recognize that these are not set in concrete, signed in blood, or declared as eternal vows. At best, these are solutions you are going to try.

Granted, each must agree to give the solution a best effort. And be willing to back up and find another solution if one doesn't work.

Don't let yourselves come to the conclusion, "Well, we tried, but it didn't work." Try again. Take another approach. Get different help. If you think that you have exhausted all ways of bridging your differences, you haven't.

Keep Each Other's Secrets

In facing incompatibilities and forging agreements, keep each other's confidences. Unless you are discussing the incompatibilities of your relationship with a professional counselor with whom you are working as you develop a solution, don't discuss the details of your spouse's values, goals, emotions, physical or sexual attributes, or background influences with others. As you attempt change and accommodation, keep your successes and failures private.

This is not to say that you should cover for another person's abusive or illegal behavior. In those instances, you need to speak to a professional immediately.

This is also not to say that you should build a wall of silence in which you totally negate your need to talk about your feelings, frustrations, or hurts. Make certain that the person in whom you confide, however, is someone who will keep your confidence. Many people find it highly therapeutic to confess their faults and sins on a regular basis to someone who will listen without judgment, forgive freely, and offer advice only when asked. This is far different from telling the intimate details of your marriage to your pals at the club or the hairdresser at the beauty parlor.

Embrace a Greater Purpose

As you and your beloved develop win-win solutions to your problems and forge agreements that bind your lives together for a consistency of relationship, allow yourselves to embrace a greater purpose for your marriage.

What does your marriage mean to others who know you? How can the two of you embody to the next generation the traits of a good marriage? How might your marriage inspire others? What can the two of you do as a married couple that the two of you apart cannot do?

Look beyond yourselves to the world as a whole. Who are you in the greater scheme of life—both as individuals and as a couple?

The two who find for themselves a purpose that is larger than themselves generally find a way to become compatible, live a life of consistency, and stay together for many, many years.

Chapter 10

COMPATIBILITY IN MOTION

You and your beloved's degree of compatibility can, and very likely will, change over time. Not only will both of you mature in ways you cannot predict today, but life will deal you a set of circumstances and situations you cannot presently imagine. Some of the circumstances will be joyous. Others will be painful and may include serious illness, tragedy, or death of loved ones.

Nearly all husbands and wives who have been married for several decades look back and say, "We aren't the same people."

In personality, they are quite similar. But in terms of behavior, they are not. They have learned to relate to each other in ways that are far different from the ways they related to each other on their first date, throughout their engagement period, or in the first years of their marriage.

ARE WE COMPATIBLE?

We have all known people who over several decades of marriage begin to look more alike. That's not an uncommon trend. Decades of shared food, exercise, and environmental factors have their impact!

What is also true is that partners over time tend to be able to anticipate each other's responses, complete each other's sentences, and know what the other is thinking without spoken words.

Does compatibility grow over time? Often it does. In fact, in some couples, the areas that were once regarded as areas to be bridged might very well be seen as areas of natural harmony with the passing of the decades.

In other instances, incompatibility grows. One person grows in one direction, the other person in another direction. Rather than turn toward each other, they turn away from each other. The end result is widening gaps.

Periodically, take a look at the five areas of compatibility outlined in this book. Reflect on ways in which you might make different responses to the quizzes. If your responses are different, the chances are that your beloved's responses are also different. You may have developed a far different compatibility profile. If so, are there new areas in which you need to build bridges of agreement? Are there some areas in which you are more compatible?

A number of years ago my staff gave me a beautiful present: a seven-foot ficus tree with a braided trunk. The tree was actually three trees, but it appeared to be just one. I had an opportunity to talk with the nursery manager from whom the tree was purchased, and he told me how the tree had been braided: "We take three saplings and plant them close together. We intertwine the trunks of these little trees very loosely so each tree trunk has room to expand in diameter. We don't wrap them too tightly, and we don't wrap them too loosely. As the tree grows, we make sure that all of the little offshoots are pinched away so that all of the growth is upward. We aren't creating a ficus bush; it's a ficus tree."

It sounded like a good formula for a sound marriage to me!

Intertwine your lives, but do so gently and loosely so as to give each other room to grow individually. Trim away the extraneous differences. Stay pliable. Grow upward as a couple.

Ecclesiastes 4:12 tells us, "A threefold cord is not quickly broken." Count God into your relationship, and trust Him to be part of your lifelong marriage.

Over time, you will appear as one to others. May the shade of your relationship provide shelter for others, and may the beauty of your relationship bring joy.